SELLING THE TOUGH BUYER

SELLING THE TOUGH BUYER

A Nonadversarial Approach

William Huggins

BOB ADAMS, INC.
PUBLISHERS
Holbrook, Massachusetts

Published by Bob Adams, Inc.
260 Center Street, Holbrook, MA 02343

ISBN: 1-55850-161-4

Printed in the United States of America

A   B   C   D   E   F   G   H   I   J

This publication is designed to provide accurate and authoritative information with regard to the subject matter covered. It is sold with the understanding that the publisher is not engaged in rendering legal, accounting, or other professional advice. If legal or other expert assistance is required, the services of a competent professional person should be sought.

> — From a *Declaration of Principles* jointly adopted by a
> Committee of the American Bar Association and a
> Committee of Publishers and Associations.

Contents

Introduction

When reading biographies of famous people, we often read that they are great salespeople. This reference has always bothered me.

Are Lee Iacocca and Don King salespeople? Yes, because we all are selling something. But how would a Don King or a Donald Trump or another promoter do in your territory? Probably not too well, because they work with different tools—they take an existing need and fill it. They shape the deal, arrange for the financing, negotiate the TV or radio deals, and assign clever lieutenants to make the physical arrangements. All of the things they do are important and meaningful, but it isn't selling. By my way of thinking, they are order takers.

I once worked for a small company whose owner had the world's biggest ego. He was, he reckoned, a great administrator, a visionary, and of course, a master salesman. No matter how good a job my salespeople did, he contended he could have done better. No matter how tough the selling situation, he could have made the sale. I have to admit, he almost convinced me because his confidence was overwhelming, but his ego was stifling, and so one day I decided to call his hand.

"Why don't you and I visit some of these tough accounts that the best we have couldn't sell? Why don't you show me how you can handle these tough buyers, and I'll pass along the pearls of wisdom to the staff?" He stopped and looked at me with startled eyes and a quizzical look. He was surprised and confused. He had been spouting off for years, but this was the first time anyone had called his hand. But in spite of the concerns and doubts I knew he had, his ego overcame all and he nodded his acceptance. The sales staff couldn't wait, and they quickly formed a betting pool.

I immediately arranged the appointments, and the next

morning we set out to test his selling skills. At our first call, my boss wouldn't let the buyer get in a word. Result: no sale. I tried to coach him between calls, but this guy thought he knew it all.

At our second stop, he and the buyer got into a shouting match, with predictable results. The third call was a replay of the first except the buyer asked us to leave.

As we drove back to the office, I tried to cheer my boss up. The day had been unsuccessful, but maybe not wasted—maybe he had learned something.

But did he? Of course not. By the next afternoon, he had an excuse for every rejection, a reason for every turndown. Nobody could sell him like he could sell himself. In his mind, he is still a great salesman.

Many people carry business cards proclaiming them to be salespeople, territory managers, and grander things as well. But the fact is, few know very much about their craft. Their success, if any, is derived from the marketing support provided by the companies they represent, by the mountains of calls they make, by ignoble persistence, or in some cases by the unique appeal of their product. These are the order takers of American business. They are not trained to sell, because the system does not pay for such training. Meanwhile, overseas competition pushes high-quality, low-priced goods onto the American market, forcing medium and small businesses to cut back even further on sales training.

People who sell highly advertised, presold merchandise are not selling and are not worthy of the title sales representative. The salesperson who sells Campbell's soup to a supermarket chain isn't a salesperson in my book. He must know the company's advertising schedules, promotional allowances, shipping schedules, and warehouse dimensions, but selling is unnecessary. He is a traveling clerk: well groomed, amiable, reliable, and hard working, but not a salesperson.

What grocery chain in America wants to do business without Campbell's soups, Kellogg's Corn Flakes, or Ivory soap? When you sell these kinds of products, you really buy the business with slotting fees and national advertising campaigns and huge promotions. The supermarket chains need these products and wouldn't dare open their stores without them.

So many products are presold today, so many are like the

soup, cereal, and soap that it is difficult to find an industry that has *real* salespeople. It's no trick to sell the high-profile, heavily advertised, massively promoted products. Now the *first* guy that sold soup in a tin can, *he* was a salesman!

Chapter 1

Who Are These Guys?

A selling career can be a difficult, easy, frustrating, exhilarating, rewarding, punishing, depressing, uplifting, dull, exciting, and active profession all at the same time. Every day is different, and that difference is what makes sales so much fun.

The people you sell to, the buyers, make your day wonderful and exhilarating or depressing and dull. They will make you think and plan; they'll make you study your product and learn your craft. And once you have mastered selling and understand the technical commandments of the profession, virtually no buyer will be unsalable. You will have gained a power and a talent that few possess and no one can take from you.

Buyers fall into two broad groups: good buyers and bad buyers. Quite often a good buyer is also a tough buyer. At the same time, I have never found a bad buyer to be a tough buyer. Let me explain.

A buying job is very special, and some buyers are special. Their job is demanding, pressure-filled, unrelenting, and stressful. Just think about it: when a person is given the authority and responsibility to buy the goods his company will sell, he makes decisions that affect everyone in the company, from the CEO to the entry-level employee. If his decisions are mostly right, his company will prosper and grow. If his decisions are mostly wrong, his company will suffer losses and could collapse. If the buyer buys maintenance products, supplies, or service items, the functioning of the business is his major concern. We take for granted that our office will have enough computers, office supplies, security, and even coffee. All of these things have been provided by a buyer, and all have been sold by someone.

At large companies in which goods are purchased for resale, the buying responsibility is divided among many people, usually by category. No one person could handle all the buying for a Sears or Wal-Mart chain; the mountains of merchandise these companies buy and sell every week would bury any one person. In addition, few companies would wish to invest one person with that much responsibility and power, and so each buyer will be assigned a category.

Because their power is diluted, the need for outstanding people in buying jobs is not necessary, or so the corporate reasoning seems to go. Hence, we often find second-rate people in critical, sensitive positions, making decisions that affect the direction of the company.

Buyers spend hundreds of thousands, even millions, of dollars every year, and this can have an intoxicating effect that can change an honest and sincere buyer into an arrogant egomaniac who is not only difficult to see and talk to, but who also never listens.

Yet a salesperson must remember the difficulties the buyer has in doing his job. Most work hard to understand the market, anticipate the competition, and maintain stock levels. They help in planning advertising campaigns and arranging special sales and promotions. Their ever-vigilant eyes never allow inventory levels to become too low or too high (computers help, but computers can't know what is happening in the marketplace, so the buyer must make the decisions on when to close-out goods and so on).

Buyers must zero in on a fickle public, try to guess what's hot and what's not, select from many models within a product group and get the one the public will want. Buyers have to work for the lowest possible price and terms, but at the same time must be careful not to extract prices or terms that are not offered to all other customers: to do so is a violation of federal trade laws. (Many companies require the vendor to sign a statement that all customers of a similar class are offered the same terms, prices, and opportunities.)

Buyers must be alert to ecological concerns and a whole range of government regulations. Their duties extend beyond buying, often reaching into merchandising, and many times their duties will require them to train retail sales personnel and direct some activities of the store managers.

Along with all of this, buyers must try to interview every salesperson who approaches them, and learn from them about the introduction of new products or systems. Buyers learn from contact with salespeople about upcoming advertising campaigns, and buy accordingly. They protect their company from consumer lawsuits (an all-too-frequent occurrence) and are sensitive to the needs of various ages, sexes, and ethnic or religious groups. The ability to jump quickly on a new product (and get off before the customer tires of it) is an instinct common to good buyers. The daily pressures and constant demands made of these people explain, perhaps, the arrogant, short-tempered and rude behavior many exhibit at one time or another.

BUYER TYPES
There are good and bad buyers, but we can break the categories down farther.

The Strong, Silent Type
One type of buyer is the strong, silent type. This buyer is not to be confused with a buyer who won't talk (which I will also discuss). This fellow is difficult to sell to because he forces the salesperson to do all of the work. He will not cooperate by asking questions or even doubting a statement. Those things you can handle, but what do you do with a buyer who folds his arms across his chest, fixes you with a beady-eyed stare, and doesn't say a thing? When I first started selling and ran into this type, I always felt they knew something I didn't, that they were going to reach into a desk drawer and pull out some awfully damaging information about my product. This is exactly the climate they are trying to create.

This fellow is an introvert, and above all other things he wishes to be right. He is usually not well liked by his peers, but this doesn't bother him in the least. He is a loner and will refuse offers for lunch or entertainment. He will discourage any closeness or familiarity.

The strong, silent type can be a good or a bad buyer. The good strong, silent type will study his category, research the vendors, and learn a great deal about your product or service. He might lay traps for the unsuspecting salesperson, and when the trap is sprung, gloat. However, the good buyer will not let your stumble necessarily affect the sale. He is testing you, finding out if you know what you're selling or just carrying a business card that reads "sales representative."

When you sell the good strong, silent type, you have a loyal customer who will work with you to solve problems and overcome bumps. The chances of losing this kind of buyer to competition aren't good since the competition will have to endure the same process and overcome the same scrutiny you did. And it isn't easy.

It isn't that the bad strong, silent type doesn't like people, he just isn't comfortable around others. He is poor at small talk, and he feels awkward with strangers. He has a poor self-image and lacks confidence, and he may envy the freedom and flamboyance many salespeople project. He, too, is an introvert, but the bad buyer will not do his homework, and rather than laying traps, he will search for some tiny, insignificant flaw in your product on which to base his refusal. He might ask for concessions he knows you can't give him or quote competitive prices that are impossible. This is his way of hiding from you and avoiding a protracted interview.

To sell the strong, silent type (good and bad), you must follow these rules:

1. Be completely prepared. Carry hernia-causing back-up materials, current publications that support your product, letters from satisfied customers, consumer reports, statistics, and current promotions.
2. Be punctual, neat, and businesslike. Small talk will get you nowhere, although a warm-up is suggested—no matter how difficult it may be to begin.
3. Respect his time and keep your interview as short as possible without dropping anything important.
4. Draw him out. Start a dialogue that will involve him in the conversation.

The best way to draw someone out is to ask questions. Avoid asking yes-or-no questions. For instance, instead of asking, "Have your sales of white goods met your projections for this quarter?" say, "What programs did you make to meet your sales projection for white goods in the last quarter?" This kind of question will require him to answer: "We didn't meet our projections," in which case you can launch your sales presentation, or he will have to explain what his programs were. Either way you have started a dialogue and involved him in the sale.

The questions you ask might challenge him: "I understand the company missed its white goods projection last quarter; what plans do you have for meeting projections this quarter?" Notice the question didn't personalize this accusation: "I understand *you* missed . . . ." Be careful when wording your questions since this type is easily offended and slow to forget.

The Introvert and Extrovert

I've used the term *introvert* to describe the strong, silent type of buyer. Most of us think we know what an introvert or an extrovert is. Should you ask someone, they would probably answer: "An introvert is someone who is inward-looking, not gregarious or friendly. An extrovert is just the opposite."

Perhaps, but not in sales. An introvert in sales is someone who, above all else, wants to be *right*. An introvert may be outgoing, friendly, breezy, the life-of-the-party, but you will see at some point a stubbornness, an unwillingness to give in on a point, no matter how trivial. These types have to be sold from that angle: "Mr. Buyer, your customers will appreciate the wisdom of the Valu-pak." Remember he wants to be right, to be known as a bright, informed fellow.

An extrovert, in sales language, is someone who wishes to be *liked*. He may not necessarily be outgoing or his interests external. He may be quiet and reserved, but he will be motivated to gain friends and admirers. This could be the fellow who does kind and thoughtful things for others. He is universally known as a nice guy. When selling to this type, a successful approach may be: "Mr. Buyer, your customers will love you for stocking this merchandise, so many will benefit from its use."

Most people have introverted and extroverted traits. I've noticed both traits in myself. It may not be easy to discern immediately which type your buyer is, but a little study, careful observation, and appropriate questioning will let you know.

It is interesting to watch TV commercials and identify the messages directed toward introverts and extroverts. Soap, cereal, and cleaner commercials, in particular, seem to have determined that most housewives are extroverts. "Your family will love the flavor of . . ." is a common refrain. "It's the right thing to do," is the tag line for a popular breakfast cereal that is clearly aimed at the introvert. When next you watch TV, look for these messages and see how you can adapt your own presentations to sell to the introvert or extrovert.

When selling to the extrovert, a hard close can be used with confidence. Nothing—or almost nothing—you do is going to offend this type. He wants to be liked; you close hard and he will have a difficult time saying no, just as he has a hard time saying no to any request or favor asked of him.

Not so with the introvert. Close hard with him and you will probably lose the sale. Remember, he doesn't particularly like people anyway, so closing him hard runs the risk of his shutting the door on you forever.

The Professional Buyer Type

The professional buyer type carries a name that is misleading, since he is anything but professional. I call him professional because he is usually found in large, professional companies. He is protected by a bevy of receptionists, secretaries, and assistants. He is usually an introvert and is impressed by titles and trappings. Although an introvert, he will frequently entertain or encourage being entertained—it's all part of the image he thinks he should project.

He is likely to belong to professional organizations, and he reads publications that are far removed from his status. This, too, is trapping. *Fortune, Barrons,* and the *Wall Street Journal* will be casually left about, telling you he knows a great deal about the inner workings of Wall Street and the thought processes of the movers and shakers. He is a problem to his company, but most companies seem blind to his uselessness. When sweeping changes are made, he will survive. He goes along with management, never makes waves, and he stays. He is without exception a poor buyer.

You sell the professional by impressing him with the customers who use your products. It is not very useful to grind through your presentations when you can instead have another contented buyer do your work for you. The kind of approach that will seal the sale for you nine times out of ten is this: "Do you know Mark Webley of INR? Well, Mark has bought our product for over ten years, and I think you two should have a lot to discuss. Let me use your telephone and put you in touch." He wants to know Mark, is impressed that a prestigious company uses your product, and his natural distrust of salespeople (a characteristic of an introvert) is removed.

The I-Can-Get-It-Cheaper Type

I include in my list of types the "I-can-get-it-cheaper" kind of buyer. You might think this isn't a type, but merely an objection. Not so. There are buyers who, no matter what rock-bottom price is presented to them, will insist they can buy it somewhere else for less. These types are highly suspicious of salespeople and unrealistic toward prices and margins. They will often be found buying second-rate goods and closeouts, and for this reason might be worthwhile knowing (some day you may want to dump some merchandise). These types usually work for small companies or for themselves (in small companies). They are extreme introverts who will stick with and defend their decisions even when it is obvious they have made a bad deal.

To sell to this buyer, you must dig for information long before you start your presentation. The most important information is, of course, what price they are paying for a similar product. Sometimes you can get a pretty good estimate by checking retail prices. An oblique question such as, "What kind of markup do you shoot for?" will tell you what he is paying. These types are rarely happy with the goods you sell them, and they will tell you on your next visit how they were offered a better deal just after you left. Don't believe them. They think this strategy is a way to obtain a lower price from you.

The Hail-Fellow-Well-Met Type

The hail-fellow-well-met type is, apparently, everyone's friend. He is loaded with jokes and will keep swapping funny stories all day long. This technique is a dodge to keep you from doing your job—selling. This buyer is afraid he will have to make a decision and is trying to keep you from framing a situation in which he must decide. If you haven't guessed, he is an extrovert. If he makes a decision, it may make you angry, and then you wouldn't like him. He is often considered an easy sell, since he does have a difficult time saying no.

He will make friends with everyone, and there is a strategy

in this as well. It is easier to say no to a friend than to a steely-eyed salesperson determined to get an order. "Gee, Francis, I'd like to buy your stuff, but I'm not open to buy right now," is something you might expect from this type. In the meantime, Francis discovers a competitor just received a huge order from him.

The hail-fellow-well-met type will cost you lots of greens fees, lunches, and tickets to the stadium, but not much business will result. How can it? He is trying to spread it out—he wants to make friends. I might point out that you will rarely find a woman who fits this description. Most women buyers, I have found, are tough—but fair and professional.

Selling the hail-fellow type is difficult because he is constantly trying to get you off track. He is diverting your attention with wisecracks and jokes. It seems you have to go along with the song and dance routine, and if you do, you fall for his plan. Instead, stick to business. Naturally, you can enjoy his jokes, but bring the conversation back to the subject at hand. Never forget why you are there and what you want to accomplish. While he is laughing at his jokes, bring him back to reality by asking a pointed, qualifying question: "Fred, I know your annual parking lot sale is scheduled for next month. Tell me about the plans you have made for it." Persist in asking these kinds of questions, and eventually he will come around.

Once you sell this fellow, once he knows you are serious and will insist on talking about your product during a visit, you will find him easy to sell—but getting to that point is time consuming and often frustrating.

The Know-It-All Type

In every walk of life we meet know-it-all people, not very likable types who know all there is about everything. These folks are introverts. They have mounds of pointless information and requirements that are also pointless. They believe they know more about your product than you do, and in some unimportant ways they might. It's touchy to correct them, and many salespeople simply won't try, since they fear losing their support. Nonetheless, some correction may from time to time be necessary. "Marty, what you say was true just a short three weeks ago, but the most recent studies show that . . ." is the most tactful way to handle mistaken information. If he tries to argue with you, back away. You may win the argument, but you will surely lose the sale.

The surest way to sell this type is to solicit his advice. "Marty, we have had much success with the new model B-225. It sells well, but we will be forced to raise prices at month's end. Can you suggest how we can market the 225 at a 15 percent increased price?" Also, lead into statements with phrases such as "As you know" or "As you mentioned," since these acknowledge his acceptance of whatever is to follow.

The Buck Passer Type

The buck passer type is *prevalent* and growing. Some years ago, a number of companies decided that the best way to buy was through committee. This is like designing by committee: it just doesn't produce quality results. Nonetheless, it is entrenched in many American businesses. "I like it. (Hope rises.) But I'll have to present it to the committee and see what it thinks." The committee, if one really exists at all, is a group who believes the best way to do its job (buying) is by finding fault in products and thereby not buying anything. Members of the committee sit back and punch holes in product after product. This is considered by some merchandise managers to be the strength of the committee system of buying. Actually it is a gross weakness.

You must realize how much power and energy your presentation will lose when your message is carried to the committee by one buyer. The committee members feel they gain points by punching holes in the product—it becomes a game of one-upsmanship with their colleagues.

A salesperson is not allowed to meet with the committee, so I have discovered that unless you have a high-profile product with heavy advertising programs supporting it, the committee normally will be very difficult to sell to.

Naturally, you must qualify this kind of customer early in your presentation. If you can discover he is tied to a committee, your entire presentation will change. You will have to arm him with statistical data, published endorsements, and other such supporting materials, in hopes this will impress the committee.

The buck passer doesn't always hide behind a committee. "I'll want to talk to my department manager," "Ruth does this kind of buying; she is on vacation until 1998" and similar nonsense will be served up unless you qualify this type immediately and continue to qualify him throughout the interview. Make him live up to his responsibilities early in your interview by asking an old selling question: "If I could show you beyond a doubt how my product line will appreciably add profit to your department this first quarter, will you add it to your product mix?" He must answer yes, and when he does you immediately qualify him as the buyer and the sole decision maker.

The Buyer On The Take

There is another rare buyer type, and you can be thankful this type is rare. He seems tough, but in reality he isn't tough at all. In fact, he is the finest buyer money can buy. That's right, I'm talking about the buyer on the take. The crooked buyer is sometimes out there, but I have known only one in my selling career. Oh, there are rumors of buyers who are for sale, but I believe they are few and far between.

The crooked buyer I knew worked for a huge retailer, one of America's largest companies. He ran a department whose budget ran into the hundreds of thousands of dollars, and he was a bright fellow who knew the marketplace.

I met him in his Michigan office, fully prepared for everything except what happened. I knew his category well, I knew what he was paying for the goods I was trying to replace, I knew the terms and conditions under which he was buying, I even knew his immediate stock levels. I had the gun loaded and was ready for bear.

I made an outstanding presentation. It was textbook stuff, and based on my years of selling, I judged it was going well. He asked a few questions, which I answered with ease, and then I closed. He fidgeted around for a few moments while I stood silently, my eyes locked with his. He looked away, and in that moment, I knew I was in trouble. Finally, he looked up and said, "I see no reason to change from my present supplier."

His company was advocating a Buy American program at the time, and my stuff was made in California; his present supplier was offshore. My product was clearly superior in quality, my terms were better, my styling and my guarantee beat the competition easily. I was confused by his answer. No matter what I tried, I couldn't get even a trial order. On the way to the airport I reviewed everything but simply couldn't understand the outcome.

It was almost a year later that I learned from another supplier that this guy was a thief and a cheat. He was taking money from foreign suppliers in exchange for his orders. He was stealing from his company and from its customers. Suddenly my inability to sell to him was explained.

The Real Tough Buyer Type

This is the kind of buyer who makes you work for his business. He knows the product and will discuss intelligently the pros and cons of your products and the competition's. He drives a hard bargain, but he is always fair and honest. His job is buying, and this is what he tries to do with every salesperson who calls on him. He may not buy your goods, but he will have a good reason if he doesn't. He understands that you are in business to make a profit and wants you to prosper, so his demands will be reasonable.

You gain his trust by exhibiting your honesty and follow-through. Never make a promise to this type unless you are sure you can keep it. A promise made is a debt unpaid, and this buyer won't give you more than one chance to prove you are trustworthy. Once you gain that trust, you will have a wonderful customer who is loyal to your company and loyal to you as well.

Buyers like this strive to see every salesperson who is interested enough to call on them. They are never closed to new ideas, concepts, or products, and doing business with this type is fun and exciting.

You sell to this type of buyer by following the rules of selling. Add to this truthfulness and honesty, and you have it. You must always be on your game with this type of buyer, and if you fail to live up to promises, he can be tough to regain as a customer.

The real tough buyer is not afraid to spend his company's money because he is comfortable with his purchasing and management skills. He is secure in his job and knows that money spent will come back in profits many times over.

Unlike the timid, insecure, and frightened buyer who avoids salespeople to avoid making decisions, the real tough buyer will talk to anyone about any product he might use. If the product fails to meet his needs, he will take the time to explain why he isn't buying. If he tells the salesperson that he will get back to them, you can be sure he will honor his promise.

I once called on a buyer from a large West Coast chain. I pounded on his door for months, had countless interviews, and tried everything I knew of to get business, all to no avail. I accepted his reasons, but I honestly felt my product line would do well in his stores. On one interview he said to me, "I'm rather locked into the ABC line right now, and I can't do anything for nine months. I'll call you." Naturally, I didn't believe this for a minute, but I had tried everything and sometimes you must take no for an answer. We shook hands, and I left.

You might imagine my surprise when nine months later to the day, he called me and said he was ready to do business! He became one of the largest accounts my company had, and that relationship lasted for years.

The Small Buyer

In small companies and in retail stores, the buyer is frequently someone promoted from the retail sales ranks. Retail salespeople are usually not big-time thinkers. They see things on a smaller scale than do most wholesale people. They are notoriously tightfisted and almost always view their jobs as loftier than they are.

Few have formal purchasing training, and many envy the freedom the salesperson enjoys. These buyers work long hours at low wages with few benefits and almost no security. Why they choose this work is beyond my comprehension. Nonetheless, some of these buyers are the sharpest you will ever meet.

Their understanding of the needs and wishes of the consumer is usually excellent. They spot trends, fads, and hot products long before most, and they appreciate the efforts of the salesperson who religiously calls on them.

The problem with this kind of buyer is they are normally so overloaded with duties that they cannot spend very much time doing what is most important: evaluating new products. They will rarely blaze trails with a new product, preferring to stock to proven sellers. They become slaves to the consumer, and you will frequently hear them say, "I haven't had any calls for (fill in brand); if I do, then I'll order it." There are ways to overcome such replies, but to the rookie salesperson, this response is a stumper.

Being rejected is part of being a salesperson. It is something that nobody ever gets accustomed to no matter what they tell you. Not everyone will sell products that are strongly supported by advertising (and hence eagerly sought by consumer). The rejection can be more easily accepted if the buyer is honest and fair. If he is open to ideas, but simply thinks your product doesn't fit, then the rejection is something you can live with. However, if, in your opinion, you haven't been given a fair chance to sell, rejection is a bitter pill indeed.

I've been asked my opinion about what one should do if the buyer is unfair. Should you go around him? Should you write a letter to his merchandise manager, explaining that you have been treated unfairly?

It's a tough and tricky decision. Usually going around the buyer gets you nowhere. If the buyer were a good one, he would explain to your satisfaction why he isn't buying your goods. If you couldn't accept his explanation, he would again tell you exactly what he is looking for, show you where your product failed, and challenge you to fill those requirements.

To go over the buyer's head with some vague idea of getting an order from his boss is foolish. Once that bridge between the salesperson and buyer is burned, it is virtually impossible to rebuild it. You have shown the buyer your lack of respect for his decisions and his judgment. You can hardly blame him for not liking it.

Chapter 2

Getting Started

An organized salesperson is a good salesperson. Business today is a sophisticated, high-tech affair with computers keeping watch on the movement of goods, competitive pricing, product turn, and margin PSF (per square foot). The disorganized, unprepared salesperson is at an enormous disadvantage in this business climate, and in fact cannot survive.

The old-fashioned image of a fast-talking, glib "super salesperson" who refuses to do paperwork and wisecracks his way to success was never true. Successful salespeople have always recognized how important record keeping is to their success, and although they may not enjoy keeping records, they understood that the information provided by carefully kept records is vital.

When introduced to a sales territory, the first thing a salesperson must do is prepare an itinerary. Not just a list of accounts. An itinerary tells you about the accounts you will count on to build your territory and your career. It will save you time and money, make you more efficient, make your job easier, and give you more time to investigate selling opportunities that lie right under your feet.

First, you need up-to-date street maps of every community in your territory. On these maps, locate and mark the exact location of each account. The purpose of this is to build a list of calls you will make repeatedly Monday through Friday. Unfortunately, the accounts never cooperate. Call A is located close to call B, but the buyer for call B only interviews salespeople on Thursday, and the buyer for call A only sees people on Monday. The buyer at call C only interviews in the afternoon, and the buyer at call D only interviews in the morning. It takes time to discover all this and then to incorporate it into a sensible itinerary—at about which time, a new buyer will replace the buyer at call E, and you have to make adjustments. But it's all worth it: once the buyers expect you on certain days and at certain times, they include you in their plans; you become a part of their business.

An itinerary, although extremely important and a proven sales booster, is one of the toughest things to convince a salesperson to follow, to organize, and to maintain. But I know its value, and I make this statement without fear of contradiction: An itinerary, religiously followed, will *increase your territory sales by as much as 35 percent!* Moreover, the time and money you save when you follow a wisely planned, geographically sensible itinerary will add thousands of dollars to your savings account.

I have worked with salespeople who spend most of their day driving with no fixed plan from one end of their territory to another—wasting hours on the road complaining about how expensive it is to work their area. For people like this, it is just too much trouble to make up an itinerary. I believe these people are really looking for excuses rather than attacking their territories and facing possible rejection. In their minds, it is better to waste time, curse traffic, and rail against high expenses than it is to spend more time in front of a decision maker who *might* say no. What a waste! Always remember: You must plan to spend as much time as you possibly can with a decision maker. Even if you are rejected, you gain from the experience.

When you make your itinerary, don't take shortcuts. I must stress the importance of marking a street map with the locations of each call. You may think you know the territory so well that you needn't make a map. But this small, seemingly trivial step is important because it gives you a visual overview of your territory, which can be useful when selling one account against another. I once fought against this method myself, but I was wrong. Get the map, mark the locations, draw up an itinerary.

After the itinerary is made, your next step is to make up an account book (see Exhibit 1). This notebook contains an inventory sheet for each account and must be carried into every account and scrupulously maintained. It is a record of your accounts. It will tell you what they bought, what they sold, what inventory levels they carry (and why those levels should be increased or decreased), and the proper name, address, telephone and fax number of each account. It will carry the account's num-

INVENTORY COST CONTROL RECORD

STORE NAME: _____   BUYERS NAME: _____
ADDRESS: _____   DAYS OFF: _____
CITY & STATE: _____   BEST CALL DAYS: _____
TELEPHONE: ( ) _____   BEST TIME: _____
LABEL: _____

DATE _____

INVENTORY/ORDERED

CODE	PRODUCT DESCRIPTION	SIZE	inv	ord	inv	ord	inv	ord	inv	ord	inv	ord	inv	ord	inv	ord	inv	ord	inv	ord

IMPORTANT: SALESPERSON SHOULD CHECK NOTES BEFORE
CALLING ON THIS ACCOUNT.

POST CALL NOTES

DATE OF CALL	RESULT	FOLLOW-UP	NEXT CALL DATE	GENERAL IMPRESSIONS

ber, the name of the buyer, the day and time he prefers to be called on. It will show billing terms, the buyer's likes and dislikes. He likes deals. He doesn't like being called *Mr.*

On the reverse side of this sheet (Exhibit 2) is a space to make post-call notes. The purpose in making these notes is to remember all that occurred during your call. Without help from your post-call notes, you cannot possibly remember all promises made and given, all requests, complaints, and compliments. And if you review these notes before you make another call to the customer you can then have samples, support literature, maybe special prices or terms for your customer. You customer will be impressed with your organization skills and the interest you show in his business!

Remember: post-call notes build sales rapidly and steadily!

I would like to highlight another important point: When you maintain inventory lists, you never miss a selling opportunity. You know what is out-of-stock and which products are short. Without this information, you miss sales, you miss the opportunity to build an inventory of your products, you create a situation in which rush orders become the norm, and you risk the anger of the buyer (who will blame you when things go wrong, no matter who is at fault). The buyer will appreciate seeing what is moving and what isn't, and his reaction to your presentations will show it.

So now you have a good itinerary and a well-organized account book. What's next? Your briefcase. A salesperson's briefcase must contain business cards, extra pens and pencils, a small note pad, order forms, credit applications, new account forms (if your company requires them), product or service catalogs, current support materials, copies of current promotions, address book with telephone and fax numbers you might need during the day, and, finally, a prepared bundle of materials to leave with the account when you have finished your call.

Organization results in increased sales. Let me tell about an actual sales situation that I witnessed. Two salespeople, calling on the same account, arrived within minutes of each other. Salesperson #1 was a glib, clever, and capable person who enjoyed a friendly relationship with the buyer—a tough and demanding professional. He arrived first, and so was the first to be interviewed. He presented his new promotion with excitement and enthusiasm, showed his samples, outlined the program, and used support materials to bolster his presentation. It was a good presentation, and the buyer placed an order. After the sale, the salesman asked, "Do you need anything else?"

"Yes, I need two dozen of model #7776 and maybe a dozen of model #7716," the buyer answered.

Salesperson #1 added these items to his order, thanked the buyer, winked at his colleague, and left. As far as he was concerned, he had done a good job. But had he? How could he have done better? Think about it and then read what Salesperson #2 did.

Salesperson #2 was not so glib; in fact, she was a bit shy and sometimes stuttered. Trying to compensate, she listened more and talked less (which, over a period of time, made her one of the best salespeople I ever knew). She was knowledgeable and organized. It was her second call on this tough buyer, and she was apprehensive. On her first call, she carefully took inventory of her company's products and while she waited for Salesman #1 to finish his call, she updated that inventory, compared it to the old one, and discovered some interesting facts.

"OK," the buyer called out. "What do you have for me?"

"Several new and interesting products to show you," she replied. "But first, I wonder if you realize how much money you are losing with us?"

The buyer's eyes narrowed, as he asked, "What do you mean?"

"I took an inventory on my last visit here, and while I was waiting to see you this morning I took another inventory and discovered you are out of stock *again* on models #441, 445, 447, and 449," she explained. "The inventories show you were out of stock on these same items both times. Now your inventory level has been a dozen of each model. If you increase your inventory level to eighteen pieces—or even better, to two dozen—then you won't be missing sales and losing dollars. Your customers can't buy when you are out of stock—and they just might go elsewhere. We don't want that, and that's why I have drawn up this suggested order—to protect you from vacant shelves, lost sales, and empty cash registers."

The buyer looked at the salesperson with new respect. This "kid" was on her game. She made sense, and she probed a strong emotion (fear of losing sales to competitors) with him. "Your suggested order has many more models listed than the ones I am out of stock on," he said.

She replied, "I took a complete inventory and compared it to the earlier inventory from last month. I brought your stock up to your mini-max inventory levels, and I am sure you want to add those to the order as well—right?"

"Right," he smiled in appreciation. This woman was one sharp businessperson, and you could see he appreciated her organization.

"Now, about our new products, I'm sure you've heard . . ."

"Stop!" the buyer laughed. "I surrender, add what you think I'll need. I want to see if you're as good a buyer as you are a salesperson!"

She laughed, too, and thanked him for the order, which was easily six times bigger than Salesman #1's order. In her car, she carefully made post-call notes, recording what had transpired, and reminding herself of what she would present to the buyer the next time.

This was and is a classic example of how organization assists the salesperson to gain larger orders, and how it helps to develop in the buyer's mind the impression that the salesperson is an extra employee—a helper who knows the buyer's business and can make contributions that will build and strengthen that business.

Being organized does something else, too. It gives you a feeling of confidence. You know you are prepared, ready for whatever comes your way. Nothing kills a sales presentation faster than the need to run out to your car to retrieve something. These interruptions open the door for telephone calls, employee interruptions, and the like. A slip like this simply breaks the continuity of the presentation.

Finally, you must establish a way to follow up. This takes any number of forms. Some salespeople find it effective to send a brief note, thanking the buyer for his time and reviewing the high points of the interview. Others telephone a day or so after the call. Still others send samples, product surveys, and other supportive materials with a note, jogging the prospect's memory. Whatever form you choose, it is wise to follow up on every call you make—especially early in your relationship.

There are five basic steps in getting yourself and your territory organization:

1. Make an itinerary, a list of accounts that either do business with you or accounts with whom you wish to do business.

2. Grid the territory. Mark on a street map the location of each account, and then, when you know what days and hours you can obtain an interview with each account, draw up an itinerary that is geographically realistic.

3. Establish an inventory-control account sheet for every account—even those that are not active accounts.

4. Organize your sample case and briefcase, and remember to restock every weekend so you'll be prepared for Monday.

5. Establish a follow-up system, and a tickler file to remind you to deliver what you promised when you promised.

These points all seem rather obvious, and they are, but they are frequently ignored. A daily planner is useful and can be used as a tickler file if you need only to make notations. If you need to file papers, the tickler file is ideal. Obviously the inventory-control file is a necessary part of every territorial salesperson's records.

The well-organized salesperson spends just 5.2 hours per week in front of a decision maker. Think of that! Just 5.2 hours out of forty or fifty hours per week! The rest of the time is spent driving, waiting, eating, doing paperwork, merchandising, telephoning, and more waiting. You must make the 5.2 most important hours of your business week pay off, and the only way to do that is to be completely prepared, be on time, and be ready to do business.

There are, of course, sales jobs that do not lend themselves to itineraries. Direct sales, for example. This kind of sales effort requires a different, not-so-complex organizational system. (By direct selling, I mean sales that require you to close the person who will actually use the product or service.) Usually, direct sales consists of obtaining leads, making appointments, and making perhaps one follow-up call. A three-by-five-inch card file is sufficient for organizing these accounts. Still, records can play an important part even in direct sales. One of the best direct salespeople I ever knew maintained a file of past customers. He would call them six months after he sold them to make certain they were happy with their purchase. Most people never thought they would hear from him again. (Think about it. Have you ever had a direct salesperson call you after you bought?) If they had a complaint, he would take care of it, but most of the time there were no complaints. Usually, they would enjoy a friendly telephone visit, and then almost as an afterthought, he would ask if they knew anyone who might also be interested in his services. It was a rich source of leads, and the people he was referred to had heard good things about him, so his path was made easier. He told me that, in fact, most times he never had to ask for leads. Names of friends and relatives were simply volunteered.

Some service-type salespeople send birthday cards or anniversary cards to customers in an effort to stay in contact and perhaps generate leads. The record keeping for this type of activity is a simple tickler file that the salesperson culls through each day. When the file shows a client's birthday or anniversary is a few days away, he sends a card. Although everyone knows this is an automatic mailing, most appreciate the effort. With even a little more effort, the salesperson will telephone his greeting, hoping a conversation will follow and new leads will emerge.

New computer technology is all around us, and laptop computers give us the opportunity to carry vast amounts of information with us. The salesperson of today need not have a car trunk full of files or need to make numerous telephone calls to the office for information. Information is as close as his computer.

Chapter 3

What It Takes

Selling is a complex, involved endeavor. You contend with many different people who have their own agendas. The buyer's personality may be completely different from yours, yet you must find some common ground.

There are many things to remember and many adaptations to make along the way. The more complicated the product or service, the more adaptations the salesperson must make, the more facts and figures he must have at his fingertips, and the more arguments he must turn aside. One must be able to adjust quickly and adapt to the occasion.

I have been asked hundreds of times, *"What is the single most important quality a salesperson must have to be successful?"* To answer this question is difficult. Sales managers give many different answers to this query. It is a favorite question asked of job applicants, and heavy weight is sometimes placed on the answer given, so it is worth thinking about.

Some say the most important quality is persistence, others say determination, still others feel organization, knowledge, enthusiasm, or attitude make the difference. The list goes on: glibness, being able to think on your feet, loyalty, a work ethic, ease of communication, appearance, and so on. Many of these things are important, and in the following chapters we will discuss some of them at length.

Successful people in every field will tell you that to achieve success, you must enjoy what you are doing. This is just common sense. If you dread going to work, your attitude suffers, and your performance will be below par. If you hate what you do, you will neglect learning your craft, you will fail to study your product line or your competition, and you will search out ways to avoid work. Like a boxer who stays out of the gym and fails to do road work, you will become flabby and lose the mental toughness you need to succeed in sales.

On the other hand, if you enjoy what you do, your attitude is positive, and your outlook is bright, your success is assured. You enjoy learning what your industry is all about, you want to know what the competition is doing, you discover ways to make your product or service more interesting and useful, you read trade journals, look for new product applications, and socialize and learn from others in your industry. And best of all, believe it or not, you'll look forward to Monday morning.

Life is much too short to spend time at anything you don't like doing, so if you hate your job, you really should get one that you like. If you dislike the industry you are in, change industries, and if you don't like what you do, change professions.

Being serious about your job doesn't mean you can't be lighthearted and playful. A dour expression and mood never made friends or sales. Happy, enthusiastic, motivated people are people others want to do business with. A sense of fun should be something every salesperson possesses, since it makes your task easier, more enjoyable, and insulated from rejection. But as important as enjoying your work is, it isn't the single most important thing needed for success.

Certain businesses and professions have gained murky images for themselves. Politicians, used-car salespeople, lawyers, and TV evangelists, to name a few, have some trouble getting people to believe them. This is a terrible burden to carry. If people are suspect of your every word, how can you ever expect to sell anything?

History is replete with stories of success achieved through persistence alone. But I have known salespeople who bubbled over with persistence, and they were considered pests. To be sure, persistence must be present in every salesperson who wants to succeed. It is part of the equation for success, but it is not what it takes.

Product knowledge is invaluable to the salesperson. Unless your customers are stupid, they know quite a lot about the products you are selling. If you cannot answer their questions intelligently, they quickly lose faith in you and turn to a source they trust. Obviously, the more technical the product, the more this is true. But product knowledge alone or combined with any number of admirable qualities isn't what it takes either.

The most important quality successful salespeople must have is *honesty*. And this quality is double important when dealing with tough buyers.

Truthfulness—with the customer and with yourself—is, in my opinion, the single most important character trait a successful salesperson must have. Lies and deceit will win some short-term victories, but eventually, all the refuse will wash back onto shore. You cannot escape it. Selling thrusts you into a position of trust. You are assuming a big responsibility and an obligation to the customer. He is spending his money with you, and once you are marked as being dishonest and untruthful, you might as well quit the industry, for your reputation will follow you like an unwanted dog. Never allow a shadow of doubt about your personal honesty to fall on you. Confront every situation where your truthfulness is involved to make certain the customer knows you acted in good faith.

A professional buyer will demand truth and honesty from the salesperson. His job could depend on what you tell him. If he takes what you say for truth, and it is a lie, his company could lose money or worse, lose reputation and image, things money cannot buy. Even if your lie is a small one, you risk your reputation and your standing, and you may begin a very bad habit. Your customers will not tolerate even a small lie. They will lose faith immediately. The reasoning is: If he lies about something trivial, you can be sure he will lie about something of importance.

The impact of lying does great personal damage to any salesperson, and depending on the company and industry you work for, lying and withholding facts can have not only serious but even deadly consequences.

You may remember that not many years ago, an automobile manufacturer marketed one of its car with a faulty fuel tank. The company knew the danger this posed to the consumer, but resisted recalling the car because it would have cost hundreds of thousands of dollars. Some managers in the company protested, some even resigned. However, the company sold the car without disclosure.

Thousands of people bought the cars and were served well by them. Several years went by without incident and, I imagine, the executives breathed easier. But then, one summer afternoon, a teen-aged girl and three of her friends were involved in a minor accident: a rear-end collision while they were stopped for a traffic light. Normally, such a fender bender would have resulted in little damage. But in this case the fuel tank exploded, and the four young girls were incinerated.

Obviously, the implications of the decision not to admit the mistake and recall the cars were devastating. Fortunately, most sales decisions do not hold life-threatening implications, and most lies in selling are relatively harmless in the grand scheme of things. But it is a bad habit to develop in business. It can cost market share, shave profits, and ruin your image.

Chapter 4

The Perfect Sales Presentation

If you can sell *all* of the people (including tough buyers) *some* of the time, you will have a successful sales career. To do this you must develop a style of selling that wins *most* of the time. There is only one element of a sales presentation that provides that opportunity: *creating a need*.

Many salespeople fall into the habit of me-too selling. They are fearful of the competitive nature of their business and, in a desperate attempt to match the competition, they join the crowd. They are saying, in effect, "My competition's got bells and whistles. We've got em, too!" This method will not be successful.

Similar to me-too selling is show-and-tell selling. I've seen both methods employed many times, and neither method is effective. If you think about it, you can see how feeble these methods are, but you can also understand why salespeople use them. It is only natural to defend the product you are selling, and that is what you do when you become a show-and-tell or me-too salesperson. Obviously, becoming defensive sets up confrontational situations—not a good position to be in.

In a way, the successful salesperson *never ever* sells a product or service! Does that surprise you? Well, it is true. When you attempt to sell a product, three negative things happen:

1. *You increase the stature of your competition.* When you try to sell a product, you automatically force a comparison between your merchandise and the goods already in stock: a comparison between a familiar, known quantity and a question mark. The contest suddenly becomes a personal one. The competition's product or service has performed well and contributed to profit. The buyer knows the salesperson he has been doing

business with and has probably established a friendly relationship with him.

Change is painful, troublesome, even scary. Every point you make concerning your product or service will be challenged by features of his in-stock goods. Remember, he is familiar with his stock and knows it well. He will challenge every statement you make, question every point of your presentation, force you to prove what you say. When the buyer is overly defensive he will, of course, also be argumentative. Does it make any sense to create this kind of selling situation? Of course not.

2. *You question the previous decisions of the buyer.* In addition to challenging the in-stock product or service, you challenge the buyer's judgment. He bought the stock, he made the decisions, and he will defend those decisions. So no frontal attacks, please. The most natural thing for the buyer to do is to immediately compare what you are presenting to what he has already bought.

   Try to ignore the products in stock. This is a selling opportunity that may not present itself again, so don't damage your chances by criticizing the competition (although you may, if you're clever enough, "damn them with faint praise"). Most buyers take an instant dislike to anyone who knocks the competition, and having the buyer's good will is useful, so sell your products while paying no attention to the competition. When you sell your products and avoid damning comparisons, you also avoid questioning the buyer's earlier decisions. If comparison becomes unavoidable, you always have a kind word about the competition: "Theirs was a fine model and led the way for several years. I think we have improved on their ideas—don't you agree?" Or, "It wasn't until recently that a breakthrough allowed this newer design. I'm sure you can see the improvement—right?"

3. *You allow the buyer to say no.* When you try to sell a product, you offer the buyer numerous ways to say no. He knows how his merchandise is accepted by his cus-

tomers and can point to its success. The buyer can resist your selling efforts by picking apart your product (and all products have shortcomings), forcing you into an early discussion of pricing and terms, and having you disclose more about your product than you wish to at this point. This early disclosure weakens your bargaining position when you close. If you ever get to close.

Selling a product instead of creating a need is called frontloading. It means you are betting all on your presentation, which means you set yourself up for a vulnerable close. You must develop a dialogue with the buyer. Ask questions while you are presenting your product, and try to get him to ask questions of you. The questions you ask must be answered, and even if the answers are not positive, they will create a give-and-take situation. During the discourse, strive to get an agreement early on. Continue to gain small concessions as your presentation progresses. If you do this, you and the buyer will consummate the sale together. The close will not be awkward but smooth and natural.

COMPARING SALES METHODS

Suppose you wanted to sell a new brand of bicycles to a store with many different, established brands already available and in stock. You have no consumer awareness, no dramatic price advantage, no market position, no outstanding advertising campaign, nothing to separate you from the competition except one feature—your bicycle can also be used as a stationary exercise unit. You are making cold calls on bicycle shops, so these buyers are strangers to you. First we'll try product selling and then creating a need.

Product Selling

SALESPERSON: "Good morning. My name is Scott Smith, and I represent The World Is Neat Bicycle Company. I'd like to talk to you about our newest model, the XK-5. This is the only bicycle available that is both a first-class trail bike and one that converts to a stationary bike as well. It costs just $250 retail and comes in six sparkling colors. You'll be happy to know that we have stock locally, and terms are available.

BUYER: "Sounds like a good idea, but my customers are vigorous and active. They want to be out of doors, on the trail. A stationary feature wouldn't appeal to them. With the inventory we have now, I don't think we would be interested at this time. If you have some literature to leave, I'll look it over and show it to some of my regular customers. Maybe on your next visit we might do something if my customers ask for it."

This is a standard brush-off, and it works with most weak and inexperienced salespeople. Once this statement is made, you are finished. Oh, you can argue the merits of your bike, you can show the handsome brochures, and you can lower the price, but you have failed to do the one thing every salesperson must do to make the sale—you have not shown him why he must have your product.

Creating a Need

SALESPERSON: "Good morning. My name is Scott Smith, and I represent The World Is Neat Bicycle Company. Do you have a few minutes to spend with me?"

BUYER: "Sure, what do you have to show me?"

SALESPERSON: "Some interesting things, but first I'd like to ask if you've seen the recent survey in *Cycle World*, the most widely read magazine of avid cyclists—people like the ones who shop in your store."

BUYER: "I didn't see it. What was it about?" *(You have started the dialogue.)*

SALESPERSON: "It had to do with the common complaint cyclists have—the difficulty in taking part in their favorite sport because of weather, the lateness of the hour, and busy schedules. As you know, cyclists are always looking for ways to stay in shape, and they want a bicycle-type method of exercise. Stationary bikes are nothing new, but they are expensive and are only good for one thing—indoor, stationary exercise."

BUYER: "Yes, I know they are. Fact is, I've been thinking about stocking stationary bikes."

SALESPERSON: *(Ignoring the last statement.)* "Wouldn't you agree that a unit that could serve both functions would be a big seller in your store?"

BUYER: "Well, I'm not sure. I suppose it might. What do you mean?"

SALESPERSON: "People who are really into cycling buy over

70 percent of all the stationary bicycles sold! Think of that! Over 70 percent! Now yours is a professional bike shop; your customers are serious about their sport—isn't that true?" *(The salesperson waits for agreement.)*

BUYER: "Yes, that's true."

SALESPERSON: "That means when they get too busy and arrive home too late to ride their bikes, they've got to have some kind of exercise, and they prefer cycling—true?"

BUYER: *(Warming up to the subject.)* "Yes, that is true—I feel that way myself."

SALESPERSON: "Of course. So our survey tells us two things: first, cyclists prefer cycling. And second, over 70 percent of all stationary bicycles are sold to cyclists. Cyclists want this kind of feature—isn't that right?" *(Wait for an answer.)*

BUYER: "Yes, I guess it is."

SALESPERSON: "Wouldn't you agree then that a bicycle that is a world-class trail bike and one that could easily be converted to a sturdy, stationary exercise station would be an outstanding seller in your store?" *(Wait for a positive answer.)*

BUYER: "Maybe. I suppose you have just such a unit?"

SALESPERSON: "The World Is Neat's Model XK-5. A sleek overachiever that sells for just $250 retail. It is an outstanding performer on the trail, and it converts quickly to a sturdy, indoor, stationary exercise station. Now your customers can enjoy the benefits of cycling all the time, year-round, indoors or out, regardless of the weather."

BUYER: "Hmm, I suppose it would appeal to some of my customers."

SALESPERSON: "You'll find it to be the fastest seller in your store and a favorite of beginners and pros alike. We can deliver this week, from local stock, so that you can have them on sale this busy weekend."

BUYER: "Do any other stores have it?"

SALESPERSON: "Bixby and Daws and Central City Cycle, but no one in your immediate area. For the time being, you have the market all to yourself."

BUYER: "Well, I guess I better have some in stock. What is the minimum order?"

SALESPERSON: "I'd suggest an opening order of two dozen in assorted colors—or perhaps you would want our opening special of thirty XK-5s for the reduced price of just $115. *(Ignore the minimum order question.)* That represents a 20 percent savings. Shall I write up the introductory special or will two dozen be enough for now?"

BUYER: "I'll take the special. I can think of a couple sure sales right now!"

SALESPERSON: "Great. I'll be back in six weeks for a reorder, but if you need me before then, here is my card. By the way, should I schedule you in the morning or afternoon?"

BUYER: "Mornings are best."

SALESPERSON: "OK, thanks. I'll see you in six weeks."

I'm sure you see the difference. Product selling opens the door for refusal. Unconsciously the buyer is placed in the position of having to defend his existing stock. You immediately pit yourself against entrenched products and favorite salespeople. When you offer a product, you remind him he has a store full of merchandise that has been contributing to profit. Or worse, you point out that he has, perhaps, a full inventory that isn't selling well. At the very least, you give him nothing to think about; you become an annoyance, an interruption, and he will get rid of you as quickly as he can.

Creating a need ignores the competition; it thereby eliminates or reduces the head-on confrontation of products and the decisions already made by the buyer. As you create a need for your product, a dialogue is begun. Challenges are invited, and objections handled. You ask questions, thereby involving the buyer in the process. The salesperson is careful to harvest agreement from the beginning, and he banks these small victories until he is ready to close.

The close in a situation like this is almost secondary. The buyer has agreed all along—what is he going to do at the close? Suddenly disagree? He would appear stupid. While he might deny having seen the survey, he cannot deny the survey's results, nor can he reasonably suggest his customers are different from other cyclists. Can he agree that the survey shows a need for this kind of cycle, and that customers want it, and that his customers would welcome it—but he doesn't want it in his store? Hardly.

It is important, however, that the salesperson not rush

through such a presentation. Take whatever time is needed, but move ahead steadily. Asking questions and getting validations will all build toward the closing question: "Don't you agree that a bicycle that is both a world class trail bike and a stationary exercise station would be an outstanding seller in your store?"

It is vital that you wait for validation of your statements. Don't get caught up in the presentation. Take what time you need, get the positive acknowledgments, and the buyer will look foolish if he refuses to place an order.

Realize that no sales presentation will sell everyone, and some customers will resist the finest presentation no matter what. People buy for emotional reasons, not logical reasons, and they *fail* to buy for emotional reasons, too. You create emotional responses when you build a need. What emotions? Fear and pride and anger and ego, even love and hate. The buyer may fear missing out on sales or think that his competition may have products the customers want and he doesn't have. If he agrees that the need is there, he must have the product. You will excite his emotions by proving the customers are there, the need is there, and the product is there. He has pride in his store, he wants it to be the best, and he wants to stock the products his customers want. He doesn't want them going elsewhere.

It sounds so logical, but emotion will make the sale. Remember: Create the need, develop dialogue, gain validation, and then satisfy the need.

Let's look at another example. Suppose you know the buyer. You have sold him in the past with mixed results. The account is creditworthy and the buyer is smart and tough.

Product Selling

SALESPERSON: "Good afternoon Bob, it's nice to see you again."

BUYER: "Hi, Mary, nice to see you, too."

SALESPERSON: "Bob, we have a new promotion of Sublingual B-12 vitamins. It's a hot seller now, and our promotion will let you realize almost a 60 percent profit margin."

BUYER: "Mary, you're a day late, I'm afraid. Countrytime was in yesterday and I have sublingual B-12 in stock up to my ears."

SALESPERSON: "What strength? Our is 2000 mcg and . . ."

BUYER: "They have 2000 mcg, too, and their deal is unbeatable."

SALESPERSON: "Yes, but our product is cherry-flavored, and . . ."

BUYER: "Theirs is sour apple—my customers seem to like that best. Maybe on reorder, Mary, but I'm set for now."

You are finished. You have painted yourself into a corner. *Nothing* can reopen the sale.

Creating a Need

SALESPERSON: "Morning Bob, good to see you again."

BUYER: "Same here, Mary."

SALESPERSON: "I notice you carry a heavy stock of Vitamin B-12."

BUYER: "It is one of our constant big sellers."

SALESPERSON: "Bob, do any of your customers complain about the high cost of B-12?"

BUYER: "Complain? No, can't say that they do. No, not at all. Why?"

SALESPERSON: "Recent studies by The Vitamin Research Council show that B-12, although popular with the public, is expensive because it assimilates so poorly."

BUYER: "Is that so? Well, no one around here has complained."

SALESPERSON: "Poor assimilation means the results are often disappointing; that is why so many customers shop around for their B-12. *(Notice: Mary ignores his remark and moves ahead with her presentation.)* They figure why buy it in a vitamin shop—why not hunt for the best price? Actually, I think this is a concern with all vitamin and health food store owners: Once the customer starts buying elsewhere, we stand the danger of losing him as a customer, right? Supermarket or drugstores don't have the quality, but they do have the price, and once a customer starts shopping for vitamins there, it is tough to get him back."

BUYER: "Well, I don't know about that. My customers understand that B-12 assimilates poorly. They don't expect more, and they are loyal."

SALESPERSON: "Point is, Bob, why shouldn't they expect more? Why pay for 5,000 mcg of B-12 and get only a 50 mcg benefit? In fact, we know that the consumer expects more from a specialty store like yours. They figure to pay more, and therefore they expect more. Isn't that right?"

BUYER: "Well, yes, that's true."

SALESPERSON: "If you could guarantee up to a 145 percent increase in B-12 blood serum content with a special type of B-12, wouldn't you sell it?"

BUYER: "Sure, who wouldn't? What do you have up your sleeve?"

SALESPERSON: "Sublingual B-12."

BUYER: "Oh we have that in stock. In fact, Countrytime was in yesterday and sold me tons of Sublingual B-12."

SALESPERSON: "Good, I'm glad you recognize the value of sublingual B-12, but remember, your customers are conditioned to shopping for bargains now. They know B-12 is expensive, and they are going to seek the best possible price at the supermarkets and drugstores."

BUYER: "Well . . ."

SALESPERSON: "Can you give me this counter space for at least the first thirty days? If customers shopping for a B-12 bargain know you have our product in stock at a price they consider fair, you'll want a reorder in ten days or less, mark my word. How about it? Right here next to the register, OK?" *(Mary is doing an end run with the buyer. Instead of entering into a long-winded discussion and bringing his attention to bear on the stock he already has, she works to gain a merchandising position. If he gives that, he has agreed to buy the product.)*

BUYER: "Yes, I guess so."

SALESPERSON: "Great, I'll have your order shipped immediately, and with your order I'll send some selling aids. How many pieces of literature will you want? Is 200 enough?"

BUYER: "Better make it 300."

SALESPERSON: "300 it is."

As you see, the salesperson didn't "close" at all. Actually, she did by assuming the sale, but no closing question was asked. She avoided arguments with the buyer by ignoring the competition. She addressed the competition but was not confrontational. She appealed to the buyer's emotions: "I know you want what is best for your customers" (decency and price). Finally, she closed after the close by reinforcing the sale and by asking how many pieces of literature he wanted. This diverts any last minute doubts in the buyer's mind.

Never try to prove you are right and the decision maker is

wrong. In the product selling example, the buyer mentions competitive products. They are in stock and selling. What can the salesperson say? They aren't selling well? He should throw them out? No. Instead, develop a dialogue with the buyer; discuss the merits of your product. If forced to talk about the competition, agree they are worthwhile, but your product or service is on an entirely different level and appeals to a different set of customers. Try to develop features that he may never have considered, or try a method of marketing that gives him ideas, a fresh approach. Most retailers have pride in their stores and concern for their customers.

In both of the creating-a-need examples, the successful salespeople set their goals, ignored the competition, assumed the sale, and closed without actually asking a closing question.

However, not all sales situations are the same. Obviously, not all buyers are the same either. Some will allow you to open a dialogue; others will not. Not all types of sales are the same. Direct sales, for example, poses an entirely different set of circumstances and an entirely different kind of challenge. Let's consider a direct sales situation.

Suppose you are selling land—acreage in another state. This is a tough sale since you must sell property that the prospect cannot inspect. For the most part, these are unsophisticated buyers-investors. The prospects in our examples are a middle-aged couple in an urban area. They might consider the purchase a retirement site or an investment. You must realize that you are a guest in their home, so you have to take over that living room without being rude or pushy. Both methods will once again be considered.

Product Selling

SALESPERSON: "Good evening, Mrs. Jones, I'm Bob Palmer with Horizon Realty. We spoke earlier today."

BUYER: "Yes, Mr. Palmer, come in. My husband isn't too excited about the opportunity we discussed earlier. I suppose I should have checked with him before setting up the appointment."

SALESPERSON: "Mrs. Jones, I'll only take a very few minutes to explain our opportunity, and then Mr. Jones can get back to that Green Bay game. I'd kind of like to see it myself."

(At this point, the direct salesperson usually compliments the prospect on her living room, the drapes, the carpeting, whatever. Then he greets the grumpy Mr. Jones, who is unhappy about leaving the football game, in the family room. After gaining their attention, he proceeds as follows):

SALESPERSON: "Folks, all the great fortunes in this country are based on real estate. You cannot name a single fortune where the ownership of property isn't at the core. Now, you folks know that your home is the cornerstone of your estate. It is the American dream—property ownership. In today's world of jet planes, swift trains and cars, no place in this great country of ours is too far away. That is why New Mexico is considered today's real estate bargain opportunity. Big money can be made out there by folks with vision and the courage of their convictions. For just $15,000—only a 10 percent down payment and easy monthly installments—you can begin building an estate for your children and a retirement nest for yourself. Or simply consider it the best investment you ever made."

BUYER: "Well, I don't know. I've never been west of Philly. New Mexico—I think I saw them place in the NCAA basketball finals, didn't I?"

SALESPERSON: "Indeed you did, and they almost won, too. Not to be a wise guy, Mr. Jones, but New Mexico has running water, indoor toilets, and supermarkets just like New Jersey. The only difference is it has clean air, sunshine, less crime, and endless opportunity. Now I only have a few parcels left in section 14, the most sought-after section. Why don't you and Mrs. Jones look over this map while I get a glass of water?"

(After drinking a glass of water, the salesperson returns.) "Well, what do you think? Have you selected a parcel?"

BUYER: "We want to think about it. We have a vacation coming and we might travel out there and look things over. I never buy anything without inspecting it. I don't think you can argue with that."

SALESPERSON: "Well, no, of course not, but these choice parcels won't be available next week, much less next summer."

BUYER: "Well, we'll just have to take our chances on that. Thanks for coming, and if you have a business card, I'd like to keep it."

What did the salesperson do wrong? *Almost everything.*

Creating a Need

SALESPERSON: "Good evening Mrs. Jones, Bob Palmer with Horizon Realty. I hope you and Mr. Jones are ready for an exciting evening."

BUYER: "Well, actually he is watching the football game and isn't overjoyed that I set this appointment without clearing it with him."

SALESPERSON: "Not to worry. Together we'll make him forget that game—just watch." *(Enter the surly Mr. Jones.)*

SALESPERSON: "Mr. Jones, nice to meet you. I just promised your wife that I would have you back for the second-half in plenty of time."

BUYER: "Yeah, well, I think you're wasting your time, Mr. Palmer. Marge made this appointment without talking to me. We never make an investment without carefully considering every angle."

SALESPERSON: "Of course, but it doesn't cost to listen, now does it? And I'll make you another promise. The short time you spend with me will be interesting—and you'll enjoy yourself. Fair enough?"

BUYER: *(Thawing out a little.)* "Sounds fair to me."

SALESPERSON: "Good. By the way, I haven't been in this part of town for some time now. Isn't that a new shopping center at the intersection?"

BUYER: "Yes, this whole area is growing so fast, it is unbelievable!"

SALESPERSON: "I know what you mean. I remember when I could have bought that land where the shopping center is located for peanuts."

BUYER: "You could have bought it for peanuts! Harry Jacobs begged me to go partners with him in buying the keystone piece down there, but I couldn't afford it. Heck, I wasted ten times the amount they wanted on God-knows-what, and Harry is rolling in dough now."

SALESPERSON: "I know what you mean. The real opportunity for making big money in real estate is in the hands of the big guys in New Jersey. It simply costs too much to get in on the good deals nowadays."

BUYER: "You got that right. Why this house has doubled in value since we bought it. I couldn't afford it if I had to buy it today."

SALESPERSON: "Frank—can I call you Frank? Frank, could you afford a down payment of just $1,500, and monthly payments of $95 a month, if the deal were right?"

BUYER: "Well, yes I could, but the deal would have to be right." *(At this point the salesperson has qualified the buyer, and in fact has just sold the property.)*

SALESPERSON: "Frank, Marge, you both know the opportunities that have passed through your fingers over the past twenty years or so. Harry Jacobs is rolling in dough because he had vision and determination. He saw a good deal, stiffened his back, maybe made a few sacrifices, and bought a piece of real estate that, at the time, was as remote as the dark side of the moon. Look at him now. He offered you a chance, but maybe the kids were going through school, someone was sick, you were afraid of losing your job, whatever. You made excuses, but the truth is, you didn't share his vision. You made up reasons why you couldn't invest, why you couldn't afford to buy that property that would have made you a rich man. You could see the opportunity, but you let fear stand in your way, sway your basic good judgment. You let a golden opportunity slip away, and like all of us, you rationalized the reasons for not buying. Now isn't that true?"

BUYER: "Well, yes, I suppose it is, but it seemed like a lot of money at the time."

SALESPERSON: "Of course. It always does. But the guys who build empires or just comfortable nests for themselves like Harry Jacobs have the vision; they take the plunge. As I've said, New Jersey real estate is among the best property investments in the world. Do you have a half million to invest?"

BUYER: "I wish."

SALESPERSON: "Don't wish. Seize the opportunity. The real bargains, the real opportunities are in the Sun Belt, in the Land of Enchantment—New Mexico. New Jersey is for the Donald Trumps of the world, right?"

BUYER: "Yeah, a little guy doesn't have a chance anymore."

SALESPERSON: "Maybe not in eastern real estate, but opportunity still abounds in New Mexico. Did you know that the fastest population growth is in the Sun Belt states: California, Arizona, Nevada, and New Mexico? Now you may not have thought of New Mexico as a place to live, but thousands of others have. You may not have considered New Mexico as an investment opportunity, but it is!"

BUYER: "Gee, I dunno, New Mexico? I don't know much about it. Mostly desert, isn't it? Do they have any cities there?"

SALESPERSON: "Beautiful cities, booming cities, growing so fast you wouldn't believe your eyes. Albuquerque is building a multimillion dollar addition to their airport; new businesses are pouring in almost daily."

BUYER: "You don't say! So you think we could make money investing in real estate out there?"

SALESPERSON: "I do. I make no promises, of course. All investments have an element of risk, but let me ask you, What makes real estate appreciate in value?"

BUYER: "Supply and demand?"

SALESPERSON: "Bingo! As population increases, the demand for land, for homes and businesses increases, and property prices go out of sight. Why is downtown Manhattan, London, or Tokyo among the most expensive land in the world? Because there are millions of people living and working in those population centers. There's only so much land. Now we all know that, except for the real estate big shots, property in heavily populated areas is out of reach for most people; you said so yourself. The trick is to get to the land before the rush of people price it out of reach. Go where the people are going—to New Mexico before that, too, is priced out of sight."

BUYER: "Sounds interesting but—well, I just don't know."

SALESPERSON: "Here is a top map, and inventory of the land still available. I've marked three lots that I consider the choice pieces of property. You and your wife may not agree. I've marked all the available lots in yellow. Why don't you and Marge look it over while I get myself a drink of water?" (The prospect is feeling the sales heat now, and welcomes this opportunity to discuss with his wife all that has taken place. The salesperson will give them five minutes before going back.)

SALESPERSON: "What did you select? I'll bet I know, the lot second from the corner, right?"

BUYER: "Marge and I have talked it over, and we are going to hold off. We never buy anything without seeing it in person. I know you'll agree with that reasoning. Next summer we'll go to New Mexico, inspect the property, and then we'll talk."

SALESPERSON: "Frank, are you going to let it happen again?"

BUYER: "Huh?"

SALESPERSON: "Are the Harry Jacobs of the world going to grab up the opportunities while you think it over and wait and wait? Haven't you learned your lesson enough times already?"

(Frank and Marge exchange glances. Could this be the chance they have been waiting for?)

BUYER: "What is the down payment?"

SALESPERSON: "Just 1,500 down and only $95 a month—just $3.15 a day. Sacrifice just one night out a month and you've got it made."

BUYER: "Write it up. I like parcel A-17. Is that a stream running along the back of the property?"

SALESPERSON: "Loaded with the fattest trout in New Mexico. You've made a wise selection. Now I want to use your telephone. Want to nail down your selection—a really nice piece of property. Keep your fingers crossed, I hope it isn't gone."

Analyze this presentation. The salesperson quickly qualified the buyer. When the close came, the buyer couldn't say: "I can't afford it" or "I don't want to spend that kind of money right now." He already agreed he could afford it, and would spend it if the deal were right.

Next, the salesperson developed a dialogue. Almost everyone you meet has passed up a golden opportunity, a chance to make a fortune or at least a good chunk of money in real estate, but other demands forced them to pass it up. The new shopping center near the prospect's home would be an obvious investment opportunity that the prospect never saw, although it was right under his nose. Now the prospect recalls other opportunities he let go by. Why, the very house he is living in is his largest asset by far, and he knows he couldn't afford to buy it at today's prices. He feels good about that, and at the same time, he is inwardly miffed at having passed up other good deals. Sure, he'd like to buy real estate—but who can afford it.

Finally, when Frank tries to wiggle off the hook by wanting to inspect the property, the salesperson reminds him of his past failures to grasp the moment. "Are you going to let it happen again, Frank?"

A newly determined Frank makes the move. You will notice too that when the contract has to be signed, the salesperson never mentions the word *contract*. This word smacks of lawyers, fine print, and trouble. Maybe Frank would like his brother-in-law (the lawyer) to look it over. Nothing wrong with the contract, but the salesperson knows that delay means second thoughts and maybe no sale.

When an individual makes a major purchase, he is sometimes infected with buyer's remorse. The buyer starts thinking and worrying about how this purchase will affect his life and finances. He talks it over and absorbs all the negative thinking of his friends and relatives, and this, coupled with his normal procrastination will mean the end of the sale.

Therefore, everything must be as positive as possible. Instead of saying, "I'll just draw up the contract," the salesperson says, "let's get the paperwork out of the way," thereby making the contract a trivial detail. No longer is it a mysterious and confusing legal instrument.

But this sale isn't over. The next day Frank will start to rethink the entire idea of buying property in a state miles from his home. Marge will read an article about the extended drought in New Mexico; Frank's co-workers will input their negative thoughts and tell horror stories of land swindles and huge losses they have heard about. This is when the salesperson cements the sale. The next evening he telephones the Jones' household. He advises them that their credit has been approved. He joyously announces that he was able to nail down parcel A-17, and he congratulates them on making the wisest decision they've ever made. He might say something like, "You know in this business, you sometimes meet people you immediately connect with. I felt that way about you and Marge, Frank. I was so worried you would—well, to tell you the truth, I thought you might let it slip away again. I was praying you wouldn't, but I see so many nice people who can't or won't make a business decision. Like I said, that is the difference between the movers and shakers and the also-rans. I'm really proud of you and Marge. Congratulations." This is the close after the close. It locks the sale up tight, makes the buyer feel good again, and keeps the door open for referrals.

When we look at both presentations, we see how product selling began with a me-too approach. The seller failed to qualify the prospect, and therefore he failed to create a need in the mind of the prospect.

Selling in this situation usually means you have one shot. If you fail to sell them when they agree to an appointment, you can almost be guaranteed they will never buy. This is one of the reasons direct salespeople are usually such outstanding closers. They have one chance at the sale, and they make the most of it. They follow all the points of selling, and they close hard.

The salesperson has followed the guidelines of a proper sale, and most important, a need was also created and filled. The prospect was qualified as a legitimate buyer. He acknowledged that he could afford a $1,500 down payment, $95 per month, and that he would commit to that expenditure if the deal were right.

From the foregoing examples, you can see why it is necessary to sell a concept, and create a need. The need, although obvious to you, may be totally hidden to the buyer. Remember, always get agreements from the prospect as you move through your presentation. Once they are obtained, once the prospect begins agreeing to points of your presentation, the close is almost sure to result in a sale.

I will discuss other sales situations in the following chapters, but to summarize this chapter, let me advise you to simply remember the following:

1. Create a need in the mind of the buyer.
2. Gain validation for points of your presentation.
3. Ignore the competition as much as possible.
4. Develop a dialogue with the prospect.
5. Ask questions to get your prospect involved.
6. Wait for positive answers.
7. Try to close hard but be unthreatening and unobtrusive.
8. Ask for something other than the order itself (special display space, for example) that will, when granted, assure the sale.

Chapter 5

Silence Is Golden — Sometimes

In the previous chapter, we saw how to begin a dialogue with the buyer. If you can get the buyer to talk, the chances are very good that the sale will be made. But you must direct the dialogue, and you must be in control of the sales situation. Being in control does *not* mean you do all the talking—or even most of it. It means that you guide the conversation. Buyers might rattle on about their kids at college, the status of the local football team, or the price of pork bellies. As a professional salesperson you ask a question here or make a comment there to redirect the conversation to the subject at hand: what you are selling. Asking questions is the best way of doing this, since it forces the buyer to concentrate on your product to answer the question. If the answer to the question is negative, don't be discouraged. Knowing the prospect's opinion allows you to deal with an objection that could later cause you problems or destroy the sale.

Asking questions causes a number of good things to happen: You are forced to listen, and you learn what the buyer really wants. Perhaps he will sell himself without your having to close at all.

Many salespeople feel uncomfortable unless there is constant talking even though the conversation might be headed nowhere. They panic and rush to fill the void by jamming in every feature they can think of. However, the buyer detects uncertainty and desperation. Perhaps, the buyer's silence was needed to decide how much he wanted to stock, or he might have been thinking about how to display the merchandise. If the salesperson suddenly babbles nonsense, the buyer now becomes suspicious.

If you control the sales situation, however, you will say nothing during this time. It may seem like hours to you, but remember, it probably seems just as long to him. Let him stew; let him think. The one who speaks first loses.

When you follow this advice, one of three things will happen:

1. He will say OK and give you a purchase order.
2. He will ask a positive question such as, "Can you give me 2/30?" or "Will you guarantee the sale?" or some other last-minute attempt to get something extra.
3. He will say no.

Do not fear these last two situations. Let me show you why.

"Will you guarantee the sale?" When he asked the question, he had already mentally committed to buying the merchandise. The buyer is now trying to sweeten the deal in his favor. That's OK. It's part of the game. Let's suppose there is nothing you can give. Don't fret; the order is yours. His reply will be something like: "All right, I'll need two dozen for each store."

Now be absolutely certain you shut up and write the order. I've seen salespeople continue to talk after the buyer agreed to buy, and I've seen that scenario end up in a lost sale many times.

What if he asks for something you *can* give him? Should you give something you really don't have to? The smartest way and the fairest way is to combine granting something extra with getting something extra. For instance, "Can you give me an extra thirty days billing?"

"Larry, you have me stretched out pretty good right now. You are getting a great deal as it is, but I want the business. I'll tell you what I'll do. What were you planning for each store?" (Don't mention any specific amount, such as a dozen for each store.)

"I'll need two dozen for each store."

"Make it three dozen per store, and I'll give you an extra thirty days billing."

By asking for an extra dozen per store, you may get the increase, but if you don't, you will still get the two dozen per store he has already stated he needs.

Now then, suppose the buyer says no, he doesn't want your product: "No, I don't think so. Maybe next time. If you have literature, leave it, and I'll look it over."

You respond, "Larry, I hope you'll be patient with me, but when I present this program, when the buyer and I agree on key points throughout the presentation, and then he says, no, well, I can only guess that somewhere along the way, I messed up—somewhere I didn't answer a question or cover a point properly or completely. Now let's quickly review this together. When I asked if you agreed that Bright Visions was the kind of product your customers were looking for, you answered yes. And when I pointed out that Bright Visions filled a need in your store and that at this price, there is no competition, you agreed again—isn't that true?" (Wait for him to answer yes.) "Finally, I asked if you felt Bright Visions was at a price your customers would consider fair, and again you answered yes. Isn't that right?" (Again, wait for his yes answer.)

"Well, then I really don't understand. If this is the kind of product your customers want and if you have nothing to compare it with and if the price is fair, what is it I haven't explained?" This is nailing the buyer, and maybe you want to ease up a tad. Take a little blame yourself. "I ran through that part about the extended warranty pretty quickly. I apologize. Let me review that again—and please ask any questions as I go along."

Now you start to review the entire presentation. But the buyer will always stop you at some point and blurt out his objection: "I've heard Bright Visions has a lot of service problems. I don't need that kind of hassle."

Good! Now you can handle what is holding up the sale: "That was an unfounded and poorly researched complaint given to the first production models of Bright Visions. We had connector problems, but that has been completely overcome; in fact, we've just won a major award for quality and carefree operation from the major industry publication, *News and Views*. I'm surprised you haven't read it. By the way, our guarantee is the strongest in the industry and covers all parts and labor. Now is there anything else that concerns you?"

Do you see how dialogue can help you to sell? Do you understand how handling objections, actually digging for them, puts you in control? Like any relationship, you must be able to talk and discuss your differences. Once you know what the problems are, you can solve them. Get the objections out in the open. Get him to talk about them.

PROBLEM SOLVER OR PROBLEM?
Mistakes will happen. You may promise Monday morning deliv-

ery, but the truck company doesn't cooperate. You might make any number of guarantees, all in good faith, and have them all broken by people beyond your control. It is best, of course, to qualify your promises and make everything as clear as possible. But people hear what they want to hear, and no matter what you do, you'll end up with egg on your face from time to time.

One of the most common promises is your guarantee that the product is going to run off the shelves. You're sure it will; it's selling well in similar stores, so you feel certain it will in every location. On your next visit, you notice the entire shipment is still sitting on the shelf—not one unit sold.

The natural reaction is to ignore the stock problem and hope the buyer hasn't noticed. The ignore-it-and-it-will-go-away school of merchandising doesn't work. If you divert his attention and allow the problem to build, you will find that in the not-too-distant future, his attention will very much be riveted on the slow-moving merchandise, and the problem will become bigger and more significant.

Instead of ignoring slow-moving goods, recognize them for the opportunities they are. Yes, opportunities. If you see that something you sold a retailer is backing up in the store, point it out to the customer! Take the initiative: "Sheldon, I'm not at all happy to see that you haven't sold even one unit from that order I wrote last time. Why haven't you?" An approach like this does two things: *first*, it actually makes the customer defensive! He recognizes his responsibility to sell the merchandise in his store. After all, he owns the goods; it is his responsibility to sell them. When you ask why he hasn't done this, you shift the blame from your product to his selling efforts.

Second, by discussing the problem, you can ask for something from the customer. "Alice, I want to see this product sell the way it sells all over my territory. I sold it to you because it is a wonderful product with great utility. Let me ask you: What do you remember about this product? Sell it to me." Don't think this response is too brash. Nine times out of ten the customer has forgotten why she bought the product and, as a result, she doesn't know how to resell it to the consumer. She will react well and will appreciate your being interested in helping her become a better retailer. Suggest ways to stimulate sale of your products. Work for better shelf position, arrange stack displays, see if the retailer will set up a display window, schedule a retail sales training meeting. Become a partner with your customer. These things will have a positive influence on your product movement.

Here's a true story that dealt with a similar situation. I called on a store with my top salesman. It was a large and busy operation, and worth almost $200,000 in annual sales to us. As we entered the office, my salesman greeted a man seated behind a large, cluttered desk.

"I'm really busy, Guy," the man said. "I'm taking over all the buying as of today!" My salesman smiled, and cheerfully replied, "That's great Hector, I look forward to working with you."

Then Guy introduced me and started his sales presentation, but Hector stopped him by saying, "I don't know how great you're going to think it is when I tell you I'm cutting back your line 50 percent! You see, half of your stuff sells well, the other half sits. I'm going to keep the hot-selling stuff and drop the dogs. In the long run, you'll do better, since you will gain sales because of a faster turn." Naturally, my salesman and I both knew this wasn't true, and wanted to keep as many stock keeping units (SKUs) on the shelves that we could.

The salesman (and he was a good one) tried desperately to convince the new buyer that he should keep the stock mix in place, but he was getting nowhere. I hadn't spoken a word since being introduced. The salesman turned to me and asked me what I would advise Hector. "I would not only keep the line, I would expand it," I said. "Our products are the best selling on the market." The buyer wasn't impressed: "I can understand your saying that, but facts are facts."

"Hector, who did the buying before you took it over today?"

He told me his mother had been the buyer since the store first opened. She and her husband, his late father, started the chain together. His father handled the financial part of the business, but Hector pointed out it was his mother's knowledge and zeal that made the operation so successful.

"I suppose your mother is glad to be relieved of the buying responsibility since she doesn't know a great deal about what the customers want—huh?"

Hector looked at me with disbelief. "Are you kidding? My mother knows the customers of our stores better than anyone."

Now it was my time to look surprised. "Oh? Well, then

your mother doesn't know about product, is that it?" My sales-man squirmed, but said nothing. The buyer shook his head again in disbelief and maybe a little annoyance, "She knows more about product than any of us will ever know."

He had fallen into the trap I had set for him. "Then you have me completely confused, Hector. You said half of our prod-ucts sell well and half just sit there—isn't that what you said?"

"Yes, that's what I said. And because of it, I'm dropping half your line—the slow stuff, but I'll keep the fast-selling products."

"Hector, if your mother, who bought all this merchandise, knows product and knows what your customers want, why does only half of our goods sell? She bought it all—what you're say-ing is she was wrong half of the time! Either she doesn't know product or she doesn't know her customers. Right?"

"Well, no, I'm not saying that at all."

"Hector, your mom bought this stock—all of it. When she decided to buy, she related it to specific customers. She said to herself, 'This is something Mr. Green will want, Gladys has been asking about this, and Ms. Smith will love it, too.' She knew there was utility in all the products she bought. She surely didn't buy a product thinking it wouldn't sell! Right?"

"Right, I've heard her relate buying products to benefit cer-tain customers," Hector replied.

"Of course, by the time the goods got here, she forgot *why* she bought some of them. She put out the product and tried to let it sell itself. Hector, it won't sell itself. You have to show Mr. Green and Ms. Smith these products. You have to explain how they will benefit by using them. New products should be intro-duced just like new salespeople, new prices, or new policies."

Hector listened as I continued. "Now I want you to take every slow seller in this store and pay extra attention to it. I want you to treat them as if they just arrived. To start with, let's have a small display table for new arrivals—tie in one product to the next, and relate how these products can benefit specific custom-ers—just as your mother must have done when she first bought them. While Guy and I are with you, I would like you to ask questions about products you don't understand, and I would like to hold a mini-sales meeting with all your people as soon as possible so they will know about these slow sellers."

Hector looked at us with some surprise. "You know, you're

absolutely right. I never thought of the stock condition in that way. We bought these products knowing they would sell, knowing they had appeal for specific customers, and that hasn't changed; we changed. We forgot why we bought these products, and we forgot to offer them to the customers they will most benefit. Will you spend some time helping us set up a New Product Center? I'd like to sit in on your training session with the staff." He bought our new product introductions and we spent the entire day teaching his staff about our products, and helping to decorate the window displays. He even helped to sell some consumers. Our sales in that store (already an excellent account), showed a 47 percent increase that year!

As you can see from the preceding example, an aggressive, forthright handling turned a negative into a positive. If we had accepted his early decision or if we had tried to argue against his initial belief, we would not have developed a strong customer with the right attitude. Remember, when you sell something for resale, you sell to the buyer and to his customers. He is mentally selling the product to specific customers long before he commits to buying your product. If the merchandise doesn't sell through, he is at fault. Your job is to help him get back on track, to realize why he bought the merchandise and for whom. So I repeat: Never avoid problems. Anticipate them. Be a problem solver, and you won't have a problem.

MAKING DECISIONS

Making decisions is a lonely, scary business, and consequently many people avoid it. Most of us have heard of buyer's remorse when a buyer has second thoughts after a purchase. Direct salespeople deal with buyer's remorse regularly. There are also pre-buying blues, a condition that prevents many buyers from buying. They get right up to decision time, they agree with the salesperson from the beginning of the presentation to the end, and then they back away. The professional salesperson recognizes the symptoms and knows how to deal with them.

What are the symptoms? Basically, the buyer cannot verbalize why he won't buy. When asked, he will shake his head, and give you a silly nonreason for not buying. "I don't know. I'm just not sure. Call me in a few days." Never accept this kind of an answer. What is going to happen in a few days that hasn't happened already? What information will he gain in a few days that will better equip him to make a decision? It may be difficult for you, but isn't it better to know now whether or not your presentation will result in a sale?

If you go back over your presentation step by step and ask the right questions, you will discover the cause for stalling. This is another reason it is important to gain validation as you make a sales presentation. But what if the buyer still balks?

A LESSON TO REMEMBER

I remember when I had my first case of prebuying blues. I was sixteen and had worked for three summers, two Christmas vacations, and countless weekends at some of the world's most miserable jobs. I saved every penny I could and asked for cash presents at birthdays and Christmas. Finally, I had saved $400. I carried the money with me at all times—in cash. I never even thought of opening a checking account, since I enjoyed whipping out the roll and showing my friends. It was an innocent time, but I'm still amazed I wasn't mugged. I used to spend hours studying the newspaper ads and walking past used-car lots, fantasizing about the fun I would have in a new car. My friends became a part of this adventure, too. They would spot cars for me and give their opinions and suggestions. Finally, when I had gathered enough money, I announced I would buy the car the following Saturday. Several of my buddies asked to go along, but I didn't want distractions. I was going to make the decision alone.

Saturday I walked to the used-car lot. Sauntering in I searched for the car I had in mind. I finally spotted it—a dark blue, four-door Buick Roadmaster. I headed straight for the car. A salesman intercepted me halfway to my dream car. After introductions, he asked if I had anything special in mind. I had been coached on how to act, so I answered no.

The guy knew my young heart was set on the blue sedan, and he guided me toward "Old Blue."

He didn't say much, but answered my questions politely. He treated me with respect and concern. He quickly qualified my ability to pay and my willingness to buy and pointed out features that a young boy would love. The car had over 100,000 miles on the odometer, the vent windows wouldn't close, the rear window was cracked, the headliner sagged, and there were holes in the floormats. The right front fender had a dent, and the truck wouldn't lock. I slid behind the wheel. The seats had a rank odor, and the window crank on the passenger side was missing, as was the cigarette lighter. The gas gauge didn't work, and one wiper blade was missing. It was the most beautiful car I had ever seen.

The salesman invited me to "take it for a spin." I drove around the block several times, thrilled at the throbbing of the engine and the obvious power it had. Honking the horn, testing the brakes, playing the radio, and exploring all the wonders of the car was marvelous. I couldn't wipe the smile off my face.

As I reapproached a curious thing happened. I began to worry. I started to ask myself questions, and wondered about its imperfections. Afterall, I hadn't looked at another car, and I had a list of ten others I had planned to see. Still, this was everything I had ever wanted. By the time I arrived back at the lot, I was torn by indecision and determined to wait.

"It's a beautiful car, isn't it?" he asked. I nodded noncommittally. He asked if I liked the car and I admitted I liked it. Then he drew a word picture of my girlfriend and me taking a drive that very night. That almost did it, but I was struggling with the realization that the roll of bills I had grown so fond of would soon be gone. For the first time I realized that I'd have to pay for gas, insurance, oil, and repairs. I just wasn't sure. The salesman invited me into the office and began to write out the contract. I babbled on about Lord knows what, but the salesman didn't say a word. When he was finished writing he looked up. Still he didn't speak.

"The mirror," I blurted, "I hate the side mirror."

He asked, "What is it you hate so much about the mirror, Bill?"

"It's round. I hate round mirrors."

"You prefer rectangular mirrors?"

I nodded vigorously.

He shoved the contract across the desk to me and indicated where I should sign. "Bill, I'm having your car washed and a rectangular mirror put on right away. It will be ready in a few minutes."

I signed. What else could I do? It was easier to buy the

car—besides, deep down I wanted it. He had nudged me just a bit, but it was enough.

I loved that car and it served me well for several years, but it took me some time to realize that I had really bought a mirror—with a car attached.

I hope you can learn from this story. If you stay quiet, the reluctant buyer (who may not be all that reluctant) will either tell you what is really bothering him, or he will give you some petty reason for not buying, a reason that can easily be handled. Either way you win.

One last point: When you close a tough buyer, always try to have something in reserve, something you can bring to the table to nail down the sale. You may not need it, but it's good to have a safety net. You'll remember that the professional salesperson asks questions to direct and guide the sales situation. And after he closes, he shuts up. If you hold your tongue the buyer may ask for something extra. That something extra can cement the sale. He asks, "Can you give me an extra 30 days billing? After all, this is a sizable order and I'll need extra time to pay." You know he doesn't need the extra time, but he might have to convince his merchandise manager that he made a good deal. So give him something. "Jerry, you are a tough guy. I admire you. But I can't carry you for more than 30 days. Tell you what. Give me the P.O., and I'll give you an extra two percent—if you pay in ten days!" Now this is a fair deal for you and for him. You give something, and he gives something. He wanted to buy all along, but needed a little extra something. He got something extra and you get the sale. The tricky part of this maneuver is not to do it consistently, and *never* let the buyer know you had that extra two percent all along. If you do, he will always squeeze you.

On the other hand, if you give something extra, and it isn't necessary to make the sale, it's a good idea to call your buyer an hour or so after you've left his office. "Norm, I just called the office and got you an extra two percent off the invoice. We appreciate your support, and just wanted to say thanks." Can you imagine the impact that can have on a buyer who has *already* given you the order? Can you imagine the trust you build by offering something you didn't have to?

SUMMARY

Listen to your prospects. Asking questions forces you to listen. You learn what the buyer really wants, you discover the real reason he is saying no, and you allow him to sell himself. You control and direct a sales interview. If you ask questions that cannot be answered by a yes or a no, you will start the buyer talking.

Never fear a negative reply. Many times the no means, "Convince me some more." A turn-down is an opportunity to discover where you failed to convince, and a chance to determine what the buyer really wants.

Chapter 6

Selling Mechanics

Selling is made up of definite and specific parts. I call the parts the mechanics of selling. They are important to every salesperson.

All too often salespeople attend a sales meeting, read a book, or receive a lecture about selling and, determined to do better, we make calls "by the book." To our surprise, we find that the things we've read actually work! But after a week or so, we get tired of hearing ourselves saying the same things over and over again. Everyone has heard this, we think, so we begin to cut corners. Slowly we slip back to the ineffective salespeople we were. This is why I insist all salespeople take a few moments to themselves before each call. Review notes from your last visit and set goals for your interview. I know it sounds simple (and it is) but most salespeople make calls without a clear agenda. Lack of a clear agenda develops poor selling techniques.

There are four parts to selling: the warm-up, the qualification, the presentation, and the close. (There is also an after-close stage that is not always used, but that is vital in some situations.) If you pay attention to each part before every call, you will find your sales growing steadily. Moreover, your sales-to-calls ratio will improve. Let's take a look at each part of a sale, and discover how each affects a sale.

THE WARM-UP
Many of the secrets of good selling are nothing more than common sense. If you were invited to a party and wanted to meet new people, you would smile at everyone, show that you were friendly, and introduce yourself to all. To get a conversation started, you might compliment a new acquaintance, ask something about him, and listen. These same rules apply to the warm-up part of a sale, too.

Suppose you are calling on a new account. You've heard the buyer is tough. All the power is with the buyer. He has been getting on without you just fine, and he is reluctant to even consider changes that will upset the status quo.

If you plunge ahead with your presentation, it would be like meeting someone for the first time and, assuming he will be fascinated with your work, launching into the details of your job. Obviously, that is presumptuous. Instead, recognize that the situation needs an icebreaker, a build-up to a friendship or a cordial relationship.

The purpose of the warm-up is to warm the atmosphere in a sales situation. In addition, a warm-up might well develop intelligence that will assist you in the sales presentation. Once again you use questions to begin a dialogue. Warm-up questions should have substance. A remark about the weather or what the local team did yesterday will usually draw a short reply. Suppose you see golf trophies in your prospect's office. A remark such as, "A beautiful day for golf—have you played the new Bear River Course?" will set the tone, and probably start a friendly conversation. People like talking about themselves, their families, their hobbies, and their business. But remember, you must *earn* the right to hear this information, and you do that by asking questions. The manner in which a person responds to your questions will direct further conversation.

You must be careful with flattery. Although it is true all people respond favorably to honest compliments, an obvious attempt at gaining the buyer's favor in this way can be disastrous. Therefore, be careful how you couch your language. For instance, "This is a beautiful marlin; you must be a great fisherman," might be construed as a wisecrack or an obvious effort to gain favor. Whereas, the same question asked in this manner will be received well: "What a beauty that is (indicating the fish); I caught a smaller one just last fall in Cabo." The latter statement will encourage conversation, and the buyer might well ask about your fish. Now you have a conversation going, and a friendly tone established. Remember that a warm-up is part of *every* sales presentation—not just presentations to new clients. The longer you have known the buyer, the easier it is to know his interests and to begin a conversation. After a relatively short warm-up, you move to the second point in a sale.

THE QUALIFICATION

Nothing is more disquieting than to spend your valuable time with someone you believe is the buyer, only to find out that he is completely divorced from any decision making. You have wasted your time on someone who cannot order your products. And when the second presentation is made to the proper person, it is flat, unemotional and anticlimatic.

Talking with clerks, retail salespeople, secretaries, and receptionists can be valuable but normally none of these people have the authority to buy. Cultivate their good will, educate them as to the value of your product or service, but understand their limitations. Qualify each of them because, in rare instances, assistant buyers and even some secretaries or clerks can authorize purchases. If you follow the steps of a proper sales presentation, you will never make the mistake of trying to sell someone who cannot buy, simply because of the qualification.

"Mr. Gibson, am I right in assuming you make all buying decisions for electrical connectors?" This is a direct and perfectly acceptable way of determining if you are talking to the proper party. But don't stop there! Suppose Mr. Gibson always consults with the production manager before he changes vendors? Gibson answers, "Yes, I buy the electrical connectors," and you plow ahead. When you try to close, he tells you, "Mr. Farnsworth, our production chief, likes to review any vendor changes. I'll discuss this with him, and get back to you next week." You can see how deflating and defeating this is.

Therefore, even when the buyer admits that he is the decision maker, push for more confirmation. "Is there anyone else who might benefit by sitting in on our conversation? Or anyone with whom you consult before buying?" Should you get a no answer to these questions, then you can be pretty sure you have the decision maker.

Never ask questions that set you up for rejection, such as: "Do you have open-to-buy this month?" If he has a full calendar and wants to get rid of you, all he must answer is, "No, I don't." You are shut out completely and immediately. Instead, an oblique question, "If our program satisfies what you are looking for, can you schedule us to be included in the Washington Day promotion?" This accomplishes two things: it qualifies that he has open-to-buy monies, and it forces him to either tell you immediately that he has no interest in your line or that he has no open-to-buy. By telling you he has no interest, you can now probe, and find out what his objections are. By revealing that no open-to-buy monies are available, he saves you time and allows you to move on to a more qualified account. Either way you are ahead of the game. I make it a rule to never make a presentation unless all the elements of a successful sale are present. I see no reason to make a presentation knowing the prospect cannot buy.

In a direct-selling situation, the qualification is tremendously important. Again, by direct selling, I mean selling a product or service directly to the individual who will personally use it.

Door-to-door salespeople, automobile salespeople, insurance agents, financial planners, personal accountants, and real-estate agents are all direct salespeople. Most direct salespeople are unusually strong and effective. Why? Because they know they have only one chance at the sale. So they are stingy with their prospects, and they don't waste opportunities. They qualify every prospect. They find out if their prospect will buy right then, and they discover if he is *able* to buy. Once they have a qualified prospect, they can concentrate on selling.

To anyone who has ever bought an automobile, the question, "If I can make a wonderful deal on this car for you, would you buy it today?" is familiar. This is, of course, a qualifying question. It is meant to determine if the prospect is serious about buying a car or is just a tire-kicker. That question is, however, blunt and offensive to many people. Perhaps a better, more palatable question is "If I could save you $1,000 tonight, could you afford just $13.30 a week for the next three years?" Pretty difficult to answer no to that question.

So qualification is a time saver and a sales maker. Many times a qualification also makes an implied guarantee. It plants the perception that the buyer is getting the deal he wants. For example: "Mr. Clark, if I could show you, *beyond a shadow of doubt and to your complete satisfaction,* how to increase the value of your home at a fraction of the cost you might imagine, would you and could you afford just $350 down and only $45 per month?" Mr. Clark must either answer yes, or admit that he cannot afford it. In either case, the salesman has set up the close or saved precious time.

In most cases, people will answer affirmatively because the

salesperson has implied a guarantee. "Beyond a shadow of a doubt and to your complete satisfaction" are powerful words that say little, but sound as if they say a lot. What prospect is going to answer no?

As I've said, direct salespeople don't squander their one chance at selling. Because many selling opportunities come from referrals, the salesperson is careful to extract as much strength from that referral as possible. For instance, if a prospect was referred by a satisfied customer (a relative, friend, or co-worker), the salesperson will maintain that link. "Your cousin, Harry Richard, asked that we finance his driveway on our two-year, no-interest plan. Is that the program that would most interest you, too?" This kind of statement actually qualifies and closes at the same time.

Referrals can also be used to "shame" the prospect into making a positive decision. "Bob, your neighbor down the block has redone his home with our new all-weather siding, and he picked our two-year, no-interest financing plan. He has payments of only $45 per month and made a small down payment of just $450. Would you be able to afford that, or would you need our five-year, low-interest program?" This kind of question makes the buyer want to prove he can "keep up with the Joneses," and will usually elicit a larger down payment.

Try not to ask for too much at one time. "Mr. McClinton, could you afford and would you spend just $450 down and $45 per month for a remodeling job that would improve the appearance of your home and enhance its value by at least $10,000?" This is two questions, but you will probably still get a yes answer. If you try for the hat-trick by initially asking McClinton if he will buy that very night, you are pushing too hard. You are making him consider too much.

To sum up, the qualification determines who the decision maker is, and whether he can afford and will spend the money to buy your deal. It is sometimes a close, and it is essential in virtually every sale.

THE PRESENTATION

After the warm-up and the qualification, we move on to the presentation. Many salespeople think the presentation is the most important part of the sales procedure. They spend too much time preparing for the presentation at the expense of the other parts of the sale. They can't wait to tell all about their product or service, and because of this attitude, many sales are lost. Why? Because they forget that there are four parts to a sale, and concentration on one at the expense of another weakens the entire sales effort. This is not to suggest the presentation isn't important; it is. In some ways it is the most important part, but in other ways it is the least important. If you have broken the ice with a good warm-up and carefully qualified the buyer, the presentation will naturally flow. It is a natural progression.

However, it is during the presentation that you can run into the most problems: the argumentative buyer, for instance. During the warm-up and qualification, he will appear like any other buyer. But this is a guy who questions every statement you make in the presentation and sets traps for you. He will usually know quite a lot about your product and will have negative opinions that, unless you are fully prepared, you will be unable to refute.

This buyer disrupts your thoughts and siphons away the power and energy of your presentation. He will ask about models that will not be on the market for months, even years; it is his way of showing how informed he is. He enjoys putting you down and seizing control. This sort of conduct tells you he is an extreme introvert. His tactics distract and sometimes anger the salesperson.

Don't allow it to happen. Instead, be frank and admit you don't know everything about your industry or your product. "Mr. Washington, I must admit, I've never met anyone who understood our products so well. You're knowledgeable about future models I haven't even heard about. I can't answer your questions, but let me use your telephone and put you in touch with our technical chief, Terry Hodkins. He'd enjoy talking with someone as informed as you, and he'll be able to answer your questions."

This reply will accomplish a number of things: first of all, it will get him off your back and provide him with someone to bother with stupid, pointless questions. Second, it will tie him to the company network, and finally, it will soothe his ego. Remember this fellow is an introvert—he wants to be right at all costs—so your answer is the ultimate compliment.

Akin to the argumentative buyer is the know-it-all buyer. This buyer doesn't know as much about the industry, but he knows how everything should have been designed—and it isn't like the product you are selling. He is a frustrated engineer. The switch should have been placed on the handle, the power cord shouldn't be coiled, the packaging is all wrong, and so on.

Try to answer the buyer's questions intelligently and honestly. "We placed the switch on the power cord to remove the slight chance of accidentally turning the unit on when you pick it up." If he continues to pursue the point, you might say, "I agree with you and I'll pass your suggestion on to the design department." That should satisfy him temporarily.

In any event, it makes no sense to belittle his suggestions or ignore his questions. Above all, do not get into an argument. Be armed with as much information as possible, respect his opinions, and even defang him by starting your presentation with a solicitation of his opinions. For example: "Mr. Washington, we've moved the switch from the handle to the power cord to eliminate the chance of accidents, don't you agree that is a good idea?" With this kind of positive lead-in, he will be inclined to answer, "Yes, that's where I would have put it." But don't rest since he will have a corrective comment to make about some other feature. There is one important thing to remember about both the argumentative buyer and the know-it-all buyer: From time to time they come up with sensational ideas.

Obviously, the presentation is when your product knowledge is tested. The salesperson who doesn't know his product will be shot down at this time. So being prepared includes knowing all about how your product will benefit the customer, how it compares with competitive products, and why it is better than last year's models. Normally, the presentation doesn't include price comparisons or terms, guarantees, or return policies, but if they are particularly attractive, there is no hard-and-fast rule against it.

Always start your presentation by creating a need for your product or service: "Mr. Riggins, statistics show us that last year failed widgets cost our industry $107,000,000. I've talked with Bob Shipely, your production manager, and he tells me that you had as high as a 60 percent rejection rate from existing suppliers. Does this figure agree with your records?"

"Well, yes, the failure rate has been a serious problem, but we think the new widgets from ALCCOM Company will hold up better."

"Have most of the rejected widgets resulted from faulty o-rings?"

"Yes. That continues to plague us."

"If you could buy a widget with a six-month or 300,000,000-turn guarantee, wouldn't that let you sleep a bit sounder each night? All joking aside, isn't that what you'd like to have in your production line—a widget you can count on?"

This method will get the buyer on your side because the question you ask him is rhetorical. He is having trouble with the widgets and you have asked, "Do you want the problem solved?"

Creating a need during the presentation stage is vital and your opportunity to *fill* that need comes during the presentation stage as well. "We agree that the need for a low-cost, lifetime battery exists—can you see how the Never-die battery fills that need?" This is the kind of "presentation close," that will ring up significant sales for you.

The presentation part of the sale gives you the opportunity to convince your customer that your product or service is needed. Here, by inference, you compare the competition's product and prices, and while you are doing so the buyer is doing his mental calculations as well. The presentation often will also serve as the close. The buyer, impressed by the product as presented, will indicate his willingness to buy. In this case, of course, your job is to shut up and start writing the order.

THE CLOSE

As you will notice, each part of a sale fits into what follows. The warm-up leads naturally to the qualification, the presentation follows the qualification as a normal part of the dialogue you have established, and the close will be a natural, non-threatening, easy-to-present sequence, too.

Why is it so many salespeople fear the close? It could be because so many sales managers make such a big deal out of closing. They build it up so that it becomes a mountain to climb instead of just another part of the sale. Many salespeople fear closing because they see it as the moment of truth.

It is the time when they discover whether their hard work

delivers results. But only the insecure, uncertain salespeople, those who lack confidence, and those who haven't followed the mechanics of selling, fear closing. Almost all sales experts believe the close is the most important part of the sale, and I suppose it is. If you are working properly, however, you are closing almost from the very beginning.

I'm sure you've been told by a sales trainer or your sales manager, "Close early and close often." Good advice. But does it mean you ask for the order from the very beginning? Not exactly. It means that each of the three stages of the sale, the warm-up, the qualification, and the presentation can contain *opportunities* for closing.

During the warm-up, the prospect may tell you exactly what he needs, and your product or service may fill that need perfectly, so why wait?

"Bob, you say you're looking for a corner lot overlooking the lake that would cost about $57,000. I've got the listing on the only lot that fits that description. If we hurry, we can write the deal today." (Urgency close.)

I've heard prospects tell a salesperson right at the beginning, "If I could find a light blue model, I'd buy it tonight." If you have a light blue model, why should you waste time explaining the product or trading small talk? Don't talk yourself out of a sale.

Of course, during the qualification, many closing questions are asked as well. I call these if questions. "If I could find you a corner lot," "If I could prove to your complete satisfaction," "If I can locate a light blue." The answers to these and similar questions will, in most cases, close the sale for you. Many sales are made during the qualification by salespeople alert to the signals the buyer is sending.

The presentation will also sometimes present opportunities for closing. "The Titan forklift has a lift capacity of almost three tons; other forklifts can't match that, and our price is under $25,000!"

"Well, if it had a safety screen for the driver, you'd have a deal."

"Congratulations! We've just added safety screens to the Titan. Will Tuesday be soon enough, or should I arrange for weekend delivery? *(The buyer painted himself into a corner tough to escape from.)*

You must be alert to your buyer, know what he is saying, listen to the answers he gives you, and watch for the buying signals he's sending. He may be saying, "Write it up!"

In some sales situations, the salesperson has to close someone who is not the buyer. For instance, suppose you are selling a highly technical piece of equipment—equipment whose operations, even whose purpose, may be way above the comprehension of the buyer.

In situations like this, the buyer will transfer information, brochures, and technical manuals to the production manager or chief engineer, who, in turn, will express his needs and opinions back to the buyer. In cases like this, it is wise to talk with the people who will actually use the machinery. Care must be taken so that the buyer doesn't seem slighted or feel you are going around him. Once you gain an interview with the head engineer/production manager, and if you are technically able to converse with him, your chances of securing the business is very good. This is accomplished during the qualification phase.

I remember one rookie salesperson who looked me in the eyes and said, "I'm terrified to close—I really can't force myself to ask for the order. My closes sound so false and contrived. *And*," she continued, "I guess I'm afraid of the answer I usually get." She was suffering from a massive lack of self-confidence—and something else as well. She didn't believe a word she was saying. That is why she thought she sounded so contrived. There are some salespeople who can sell anything, anywhere, to anybody, without the slightest belief in what they are peddling, but most salespeople have to believe in what they are selling. If you have a problem believing in the product or service (or company) you sell, and that lack of belief affects your ability to close sales, change jobs at once.

As a salesperson, your goal is to get to the decision maker and convince him he needs your product. We prepare for that moment when we can write the order. Why then should we shrink from that opportunity? It doesn't make sense!

If, after attempting to close, your prospect says no, don't nod and pack up and leave. You have your buyer talking, exchanging ideas, and you are getting close to the truth. His answer *probably* isn't a no, and could well be a disguise—the real reason for his not buying could be just a question or two away.

Don't be afraid to ask why he has said no. But don't simply ask, "Why?" Instead prepare for additional dialogue: "George, I'm truly surprised at your answer. We've discussed how my product would fit into your mix, and unless I missed something, you agreed it would be a good addition. Maybe I've failed to explain something to your satisfaction. Are there any questions you might care to ask?" Keep probing, keep asking questions; you'll get to the real reason for his answer.

Always gather as much information about your prospect's objections as you can. Solve as many problems and objections immediately, and if further information is needed, information you do not have at your fingertips, schedule another appointment. Remember, rejections are business decisions of the buyer and should never be taken personally. Leave the door open for a return visit; keep a pleasant attitude.

There are many ways to close. The assumptive close is probably the one most often used: "I can have these delivered tomorrow so you can have them on sale for your Grand Opening; will six dozen be enough, or should I send a gross?" "I'd like to make a stack display right here next to sporting goods—may I?" "Can we get these in the ad in time for this weekend?" These and similar questions are all assumptive sales closing questions. When the buyer answers yes to these questions, you have scored a double victory, since he has actually answered, "I'm buying the goods *and* you have my permission to display them here."

Questions such as, "What do you think?" or "Isn't this what you need?" are subjective questions and are not closers. These kinds of questions can lead to answers that prevent you from closing.

A review close is simply a quick recapitulation of your presentation. It, too, is an assumptive close, and it is used in the following manner: At the end of the presentation, the salesperson says, "We agree the product has strong consumer acceptance, it's priced to sell in your store, and it has an advertising program to push it through, right? Good, now I suggest the introduction special of seventy-two pieces, but you move a lot of goods, so I may be understocking you. Should we make it a gross?"

The hanging, unasked question is an easy and popular way to close, since it really doesn't push very hard. "I can have them delivered in time for your Grand Opening." Or, "If I could use your telephone, I can guarantee delivery by two o'clock to-morrow." This kind of soft close really doesn't ask for anything or even directly assume anything; instead, it merely states a fact. It forces the buyer to say, "OK, use the telephone," or "No, don't ship them." Either way, you have an order or a dialogue going that may well lead to an order.

Keep in mind that you are a salesperson, and you are ex-pected to ask for business. But be careful not to push too hard; try not to be offensive, keep it light, smile, and, if you don't make the sale, keep the door open for your next visit. Finally, remem-ber people buy because it benefits them—not you. If you truly serve your customers, your sales will follow.

THE CLOSE AFTER THE CLOSE

I call this follow-up step to the Big Four the after-close; and it is peculiar to certain types of sales, in particular direct sales. We al-ready know about buyer's remorse, the condition that some-times begins after a prospect has agreed to buy a product or service. Second thoughts creep in as he reviews his financial con-dition, the length of the contract, or hears negative things from others. In most states, laws have been passed that require the seller to cancel any agreement within 72 hours after the sale upon written notice. This is written into the contract, and the buyer must acknowledge by signature that he understands his right to cancel. This makes the after-close a necessary part of the direct salesperson's repertoire.

Within twenty-four hours or so after the sale, the salesper-son will contact the buyer and inform him, "Your credit has been cleared," or "We got that shade of green you and Marge wanted"—anything that will lock the sale up. Getting the buyer to feel as obligated as possible is the idea behind showing this extra effort.

What if the salesperson encounters someone who says, "I've thought it over and decided against buying at this time"? A personal meeting will have to be asked for to wrap up the de-tails. At that meeting, the wise salesperson will not give too much additional information, since this tends to confuse an al-ready confused buyer. Instead, a review of the positive points he agreed on earlier and gentle probing to discover the reason(s) for the change of heart should reestablish a firm buy.

When the problem is resolved and the deal rewritten, the salesperson will make the after-close immediately. "Bob, you and Marge aren't going to back out on me again are you?" *(All said with a smile.)* "I called the office just now to make certain we got that special model with the power stripes, and I reserved it for you." This is intended to obligate the buyer and make it especially difficult for him to cancel a second time (which is very rare).

◆ ◆ ◆

Many salespeople don't like to push. So what do you do? Your job is to write orders, and pushing seems to be the only way to do that. Disguise the push: "Mr. Nubar, I know you like our gauges, and we agreed they will do the job. You want to see Hi-precision's new models, and I certainly understand that, but at the same time, I want to get the order registered before the price increase. Tell you what I'm going to reserve sixty gauges at the old price, and if you decide later you want to cancel, it's no problem. I can easily sell them to the Franklin Foundry at that price. You're under no obligation, of course."

This is about as soft as you'll ever want to get. The pressure is subtle and disguised. The buyer may feel an obligation to the salesperson who wants to reserve these old prices for him. *"This salesperson isn't pushy. In fact just the opposite. He said I'm under no obligation. Maybe I should get some backup gauges at this old price."* These kinds of thoughts are encouraged by this close. Chances are the buyer will tell the salesperson to ship because he wants the bargain and he doesn't want his competitor, the Franklin Foundry, to get the deal.

Chapter 7

The Perfect Presentation Revisited

First of all, I want to admit here that there is no such thing as a perfect presentation. No matter how fine the presentation, no matter how carefully planned, not everyone will buy. I don't understand it, and I doubt that anyone does. I've had buyers agree with every point I made from the warm-up to the close and then had them say no. Unbelieving, I would review, take them once again over the salient points, asking questions, getting affirmative answers at all the critical places. I would sum up making sure my prospect agreed with all I had to say. I still got a no.

Having said that, I should point out that I consider most of the problems salespeople encounter to be eminently repairable—with the right attitude. Many salespeople who say they want to improve, to change and grow, don't put new-found knowledge to work. Foolish, isn't it? Why would otherwise intelligent people fail to use tools that can improve their careers? Lots of reasons, I suppose, but generally, it is due to fear.

When you ask salespeople why they won't employ their sales knowledge, they say: "It makes sense, but I can't say that—it just isn't me." Well, at least that part is true. It isn't them, and that is what they should be trying to change. But change is difficult.

Social scientists report that the most important condition that *must* exist to break habits or addictions is the *desire* to change. Poor work habits, poor selling routines, poor preparation are nothing more than addictions—but they are addictions you can break if you want to.

Remember the feeling you had when you sold a big account? You were on cloud nine. Don't you think that shows to those around you? Don't you imagine a buyer senses your power and confidence? A famous trainer told me that horses sense a rider who is inexperienced and unsure. Buyers are like this, too. They sense uncertainty, lack of conviction, and fear.

Self-confidence comes from within; it is carried along with a positive attitude. Sales require a toughness that not everyone has. It is a mental toughness that makes a good salesperson something very special. How does one develop self-confidence? It's really quite simple:

1. Study the product or service you sell. Learn everything about it and play the devil's advocate. Try to find faults in what you sell. Research the competition's products or service. Be as objective as you can be, and ask yourself, "If I were a consumer, which would I prefer?" Once you are sure of your knowledge, your self-confidence will begin to grow.

2. Sell to a friend, a relative, or a neighbor. Tell them to be tough buyers and to ask questions that stretch your knowledge. This will help train you to answer the buyer's questions and teach you to think on your feet.

3. Carefully prepare for every call, no matter how small or insignificant it may seem. This develops a pattern for approaching every account and marks you as a professional.

The acid test for self-confidence comes at the close—when you ask for the order. If you really know your stuff, you will expect every presentation to result in a sale. If you know and believe in what you are selling, your enthusiasm, your energy, and the power of your sales presentation will be so overwhelming that few will resist you. If you have self-confidence and belief in your product, asking for the order will be easy.

You may backslide. At sometime you may start to revert to your old ways, or you may hit a dry period and find you just can't seem to write an order. Shortly thereafter, you may discover you're having trouble closing—and to your horror—find you aren't asking for the order! This is when you use the zapper. Try it for one week, and see what a difference it makes.

The Zapper

Suppose you sell industrial grinding materials. After the warm-up and qualification, ask this question: "Mr. Buyer, what is it you expect my product to do for you?" Buyers are used to being told what products will do for them. So you won't get much flack. Usually the buyer tells you exactly what he expects industrial grinding materials to do. "I expect your product to last longer than my present supplier's stuff, and I want to pay less for it as well." Now comes the zapper: "Will you need three dozen a week or will you need more?"

That's it! You don't tell the buyer anything else about the product, no comparisons, nothing. You will be amazed how many buyers will give you an order just because you asked for it! Of course, some will resist, some will want to know more about your products, some will inquire about price, terms, and delivery, and some will be offended. But most importantly, you will have broken your string of no-hitters and established yourself as once again being a positive, self-confident salesperson.

THE BUYER WHO WON'T TALK

"Who's the toughest buyer you call on—the toughest sell?" The question came from Red Frolich, a competitor and friend I've known for many years. That was a difficult question, and I didn't answer right away. The others at the table pitched right in, all anxious to tell their stories about the buyer from hell. But there was no consensus. No more than two salespeople could agree on who was the toughest buyer they knew.

Frolich turned to me. "Who do *you* think is the toughest?" I thought for a few minutes, then I answered: "The buyer who won't talk."

Let's understand this kind of buyer. He is a type, and within his type there are subtypes. In general, they are introverted and they lack self-esteem. The power they enjoy in their jobs is a heady wine for them, and many will use this power as a weapon. Some have an almost sadistic side to them, and seem to enjoy watching a salesperson squirm under their silent gaze. They are studious, bookish types, and because of this they usually know their product well. They are often arrogant, and being introverts they want, above all things, to be right. Their interests are limited and they don't appreciate small talk. They resist attempts at entertainment, and should you be unlucky enough to get them out to dinner or a show, you will find they are self-conscious in social situations.

Selling this type of buyer is never easy. It requires more preparation than with the buyer who will talk and exchange ideas. However, no matter how difficult it may seem, you can get this type to talk. This is done by asking questions. The questions you ask must be carefully chosen, and carefully spoken, for the quiet buyer is thin-skinned. Aim your questions toward his intellect—ask questions that require him to answer by showing off his knowledge. Most will enjoy answering questions of this kind.

For example, you might say, "Mr. McHugh, would you agree that the finest couplers are made from stainless steel with copper inserts? This seems to be the opinion of many production people I've talked to, and I'd appreciate your ideas." It is likely McHugh will want to tell you why he agrees or disagrees. Remember, here is a buyer who spends his time researching his product. He has fixed opinions and wants to share them. Your questions will draw him out.

Listen to what he has to say, since he will be telling you how to sell him. Pop in a question from time to time, something to keep the conversation going, and questions that will further help you in selling him. "But wouldn't an alloy tend to rust?" for example, might be all you need to say to get a full education about couplers—and a lesson on how to sell him.

At some point, you have to start selling. As the quiet buyer slows down, say, "Well, you've given me something to think about, and I thank you for your ideas. Since you believe, as I do, that alloy and stainless provide the best couplers, I'd like you to consider our model STR-5. As far as I know, it is the only coupler made in America, and I know you prefer American-made couplers—isn't that right?" This approach to the close should harvest business for you. He has been telling you what he likes, and you may even have gained affirmation as he went along. So when you close you merely continue to agree: "Mr. McHugh, what you've been telling me about couplers describes exactly how Dyno-couplers model #M151 is made. We can deliver this Monday. Would that be OK?"

Another drawing-out method that works is making a provocative statement about a competitor's product. "According to reports I've been hearing, Loring has a new grease-impactor, called GI88. They say it will last three times longer than the finest petroleum-base lubricant available today. Have you heard about it? What do you think?" Since this type of buyer resists change and is slow to accept new ideas, you can almost be sure he will have arguments about why GI88 isn't what it is cracked up to be. Traditional is his hallmark, and this should guide you in your quest.

A few more things you might note about this buyer: if you gain his trust, he is among the most loyal of customers. If you provoke his anger, he is slow to forgive. He has a long memory and will never forget a foul up or a broken promise. He wants to be in charge. Continue to feed him information after the sale to keep the lines of communication open.

Chapter 8

What Makes Them Buy?

I have asked many a job applicant what he thought was the single most important factor in making a sale. This is a big question, since there are so many things that figure into any sale. But all good professional salespeople will tell you every sale is driven by emotion. Some logic is needed: graphs, charts, and samples are used, but the emotional appeal will make the sale. When I say sale, I don't mean a reorder. I mean a fresh, new purchase of something that the buyer may not have wanted when first contacted, something that he may never have heard of before the sales contact.

While creating a need for your product or service, you must drive the sale by stimulating the buyer's emotions. For example, when you visit an automobile showroom, you may ask the salesperson about horsepower, the wheel base, the brakes, the transmission, and other mechanical features. Naturally, these things are important, and when the purchase represents a significant cash outlay, you will pay attention to them. But the things that will make the sale, the things that make you decide on one car over another is the emotion that new car excites. The bright colors, the sleek line, the flawless appearance, the new-car smell, and the purr of the engine. Our imagination paints a picture of us in that new car, a wide open highway stretched before us, without a care in the world.

If we manage to escape the siren call of the new car while at the dealer showroom, our drive home in the old car will usually bring it back to us in a hurry. Suddenly, the automobile we were happy with yesterday is an eyesore and a blight on the neighborhood. This is an emotional reaction, and it can force you into making a change.

This isn't to say that logical reasons do not figure into a

purchase. They do, of course, but it is amazing to see how emotion dominates every sale. Even the most antiseptic product or service is sold—and bought—by appealing to emotion in some way.

Examples

In the early days of television, a major TV maker was surprised to find that one of its leading dealers, in units sold per capita, was located not in New York, Chicago, or Los Angeles, but in a small town in Iowa. Month after month this country dealer was matching and surpassing the sales of his big city counterparts. The head of the marketing department pored over the statistics and demographics of this small trading center. No matter how thoroughly he studied the situation, he couldn't determine the causes for this sales phenomenon. It simply didn't make sense. Intrigued, he led a team to Iowa to investigate.

They discovered the store was located in an old barnlike structure some three miles from town. They interviewed the retail sales staff and found that nothing distinguished them from salespeople working in other stores. The prices were on a par with those in other stores, and in some cases higher. The mystery continued to grow. Finally, they interviewed the owner.

They had a list of questions to ask, and confronted the owner expecting to discover some heretofore unknown merchandising secret. "Any of you fellas have kids?" the owner asked. "Well, if you do, chances are at one time or another, they've come home with a puppy they picked up somewhere. Now you and your wife probably didn't make any plans for a puppy. You might be totally against the idea. But when that big-eyed puppy looks at you with those sad eyes, when that warm little belly is comfortably nestled in your lap, and when the family has that pup around for a few hours—well, they aren't likely gonna let it go, are they? The pup might keep you up half the night whining, but in the process it becomes a part of the family, and you wouldn't think of sending it back."

The marketing team members looked at one another, puzzled. The store owner continued. "It's simple. I let people take a TV home for a few nights with only a refundable deposit required. I let em see how it matches their furniture, where it will fit into the room, where it should be placed. Well, after a family watches TV for a few nights, after the kids invite their friends in to watch their favorite programs together the TV becomes just like that puppy dog—a part of the family. And like the puppy dog, you wouldn't think of letting it go."

The boys from the marketing team realized they were talking to a real salesman. Here was a man who understood human nature and how emotion sells. He was touching all sorts of emotional buttons in his store.

◆ ◆ ◆

I once hired a salesman who was a technical genius. He knew everything about his product and everything about the competition's products, too. He could break down and reassemble a camera as easily as you or I might open a can of peas. He read everything he could about our competition and knew what was going on in the industry all over the world. He could speak authoritatively about products that were years away from being introduced to the marketplace, and was often on call from our own repair department.

He had a few very strong accounts—people who, like himself, were highly technical and appreciated his knowledge and expertise. However, overall, I could see nothing but decline in his territory. I asked him point blank, "Do you like being a salesman?"

"I like selling when I can explain how things work and why they are engineered like they are, but I don't like any of the rest of it. I'm just not cut out for that sort of thing; it just isn't me." I had to agree. He simply didn't have a sales personality, and no amount of training was going to change that. He was wise to understand himself, and he was wise to leave sales and become a technician. The last I heard of him he was successful and happy.

Not everyone can be or should be in sales.

BODY LANGUAGE AND GESTURES

I'm sure we have all sat through boring lectures and engrossing lectures in schools and churches. The difference was, of course, the speaker. Two teachers may impart the same lesson and both may be very knowledgeable, but one's classes are jammed, while the other's are almost empty. The message is the same, but the messenger is different.

I once had a salesman working for me who, like the technician I mentioned earlier, was very knowledgeable. He loved talking to others with similar interest, but when it came to selling he was a joke. He had the very disturbing habit of lowering his voice during the presentation. When I first witnessed this, I thought it was a ploy to get the buyer to pay attention. But that wasn't the case. It was a manifestation of insecurity that was annoying to the buyer and devastating to his sales record.

When I worked with this fellow, I found myself waiting for his voice to tail off. I watched for the buyer leaning closer and closer. It didn't sell many goods. Naturally, we had many talks aimed at correcting his habit. Nothing seemed to work.

Finally, in desperation, I suggested he watch a popular TV evangelist who was preaching that night. The evangelist was a marvelous speaker and, in hiw way, a great salesman. He used props, gestures, body language, and voice ranges that conveyed his message well. He was a treat to watch, and I hoped my salesman would benefit.

The next day the salesman told me he had enjoyed the sermon, and he planned to use some of what he had seen. I advised him to continue to watch and study the gestures and voice inflections. Before long my salesman was attending other lectures and sermons. Politicians, motivational speakers, and others were subject to his scrutiny. I could see marked improvement in his presentations, and much to my relief, he had stopped lowering his voice as he spoke.

His sales started to climb; I was delighted. He joined a fraternal organization that required every member to speak before the group. He had overcome his shyness and was a much more outgoing, demonstrative person. His sales went up.

You can often change a pattern that's keeping you from success. And you shouldn't think that you have to fit a stereotype to do so. The popular image of salespeople as loud extroverts with bright neckties and checkered sports coats is rarely true. Good salespeople come in all shapes, sizes and genders. Some are surprisingly quiet—even somber; others are animated and demonstrative. All are, however, interesting to listen to, and all use emotion to sell.

Examples

You'll recall the story of my first automobile purchase. Lots of emotion was used in that sale. The salesman drew word pictures of the fun I would have in my car; he asked me about my girl and commented on how much fun she and I would have.

Suppose you are selling photo equipment in a retail store. Your customer is a young couple considering buying a camcorder. Their budget is limited, and although they want the model you demonstrated, they are beginning to feel uncomfortable with their situation. They feel obligated to a degree, since they have taken up a lot of your time, but they have prebuyer's blues. (They want the unit, but need motivation to make a positive decision.)

BUYER: "We're just not sure this is the right time to buy. It's so close to Christmas, and—well, I think we'll wait."

SELLER: "Yes, it rolls around quickly, doesn't it? I understand your wanting to wait. Let me ask you, why buy a camcorder at all? We have a great deal on a 35mm camera. Why not consider one of these?" *(This approach will cement their determination to get the camcorder—no one wants to settle for second best.)*

BUYER: "Oh no. A camcorder is so much better. Why, when we start our family we'll be able to capture the first step the baby takes, and his first words, too! We'll have his first baths on film with sound. These are priceless things we'll treasure all our lives." *(He just sold himself.)*

SELLER: "You make a lot of sense, and you state your reasons well. I can see you've thought about this a long time. But I'm a little puzzled. Wouldn't you two treasure a videotape of yourselves as single people? Your last unmarried Christmas together—isn't that something you would want to show your kids someday? I know I'd love to have a tape of my Mom and Dad when they were young and in love."

BUYER: "Well, yes we would, but like I said, Christmas is just around the corner, and we will have so many expenses—no, it's just out of the question right now."

SELLER: "Have you ever bought a suit or a dress that was scandalously expensive? You thought at the time, 'I can't afford this, but I just gotta have it.' You wore that suit or dress until it was almost a rag. You loved it, and received compliment after compliment on it, and so you forgot about that scandalous price. You got your money's worth many times over—am I right? This camcorder will do much more for you than any dress or suit you will ever own."

BUYER: "Well, yes—er, do you have a payment plan?" *(That's the signal. He has agreed to buy—you just have to work out a way for him to pay for it. Stop selling now, and work on the terms.)*

SELLER: "Of course, we have layaway, or a monthly program. In your situation, I'd recommend the terms."

All throughout this example, emotion is used. In fact, it's a bit sugary—but not unrealistic. The salesman's reference to his own parents young and in love is bound to spark emotion in both people. They will relate to providing these priceless tapes for their kids, and the mention by the buyer of first steps and first baths clinched the sale.

If the seller had stuck only to the lens quality, the light-weight body, or the ease of operation, he would have lost the sale. Emotion sells.

Emotion in selling isn't always obvious. In fact, sometimes you have trouble detecting the use of emotion, as in the case of a mainframe computer sale. Most industrial products seem to have low emotional appeal, and that is why, I suppose selling in-dustrial goods isn't as much fun. But emotion does play a role in even this technologically advanced field.

✦ ✦ ✦

Suppose you are selling industrial greases and other lubri-cations. Now this is a pretty mundane product and difficult to get emotional about. Only the most dedicated mechanic could find grease exciting, but let's give it a try.

SELLER: "Mr. Tyrone, any good industrial grease should al-low your machines to function smoothly. But I have customers who actually forget why they buy lubricants. They save pennies, while thousands of dollars worth of equipment is at stake—right?"

BUYER: "I don't quite follow you—what do you mean?"

SELLER: "As I recall a Cincinnati 7.5 ton injection molding machine costs around $500,000 isn't that so?"

BUYER: "No, it's more like $700,000."

SELLER: "That's a lot of money. Our Uni-pak industrial grease is the most expensive on the market. We are twice as expensive as Multi-lube, your present supplier. But there is a good reason for this, otherwise we wouldn't be the industry leader— isn't that so?"

BUYER: "Well, I don't know, seems to me you guys charge too much."

SELLER: "Mr. Tyrone, did you know Tucson Plastics lost a Cincinnati to friction just last week? And did you know they used Multi-lube? I'm not saying Multi-lube isn't good stuff—in fact I know they sell good quality, but the new machines are so highly torqued, they require special high-strength grease."

BUYER: "Yeah I heard about Tucson, but their maintenance guy is a clown. I've been using Multi-lube for years and never had any problems."

SELLER: "Respectfully, you never had a 7.5 Cincinnati before. Oh, you might be lucky; nothing might happen for six months or more, everything might look fine and check out fine but inside, where you can't check, dangerous wear could be endangering your expensive machine."

BUYER: "Well, you may have a point, but $22 a pound— wow! You guys are just too expensive. Maybe I'll talk to my mechanic. Call me next week."

SELLER: "Mr. Tyrone, next week could be too late. What if, because you put off making a decision, you lost the Cincy? Is it worth the risk? I put off having my automobile transmission serviced, and it cost me a new one—$1,200 against $35—the example fits."

BUYER: "Well, I dunno—your point's well taken, I just . . ."

SELLER: "Tell you what. Lend me your telephone and I'll have the grease delivered first thing tomorrow morning. You'll have those machines protected for the big weekend runs."

BUYER: "OK, I guess I might as well insure myself against whatever."

SELLER: "That's a good way to put it—insurance."

Here the salesman planted a nagging concern in the buyer's mind. He would have kept him from having a good night's sleep if he didn't buy, and he assumed the sale by asking to use the telephone to place the order. He personalized the sale by telling about losing his automobile transmission. Did he sell the grease? No. He sold insurance and protection, security and peace of mind.

The salesman found a way to inject emotion in a dramatic, interesting, and realistic way.

What would the salesman have done if the buyer insisted on waiting to talk to his mechanic? The wisest path would be to guarantee the utility of the product. "Mr. Tyrone, every industrial journal in the country has endorsed the quality and effectiveness of Uni-pak. Protect your machines now. If your mechanic honestly believes Uni-pak isn't superior in every way, the product will be returned and what you use will be my gift to you. Is that fair?" (*Rarely will an offer like this be refused, and rarely will the product be returned. The mail-order business was built on this principle.*)

Chapter 9

The Business Letter

A business letter can accomplish a number of things that may be difficult or impossible to accomplish by other means. It can reach someone who is difficult to locate by telephone or see in person. The business letter may be opened and read by a secretary, but it will always be passed on to the addressee. It is a personal method of communication, and it will elicit a response 90 percent of the time.

The business selling letter may reach customers so spread out geographically that personal contact is impractical. It is, of course, a relatively inexpensive method to reach a market and highly profitable as well.

The business letter can be a permanent record, so it behooves you to take special care in composing it. The spoken word can be quickly explained, but people interpret the written word in strange ways.

THE SELLING LETTER

We have all received written communications from companies that conduct their sales activity by mail. This is usually called junk mail, and judging from the way much of it is written, the name fits. Some such mailings, however, are clever and seductive, and I have noticed a trend towards low-profile, dignified, and effective methods in the past few years. Business mailings are targeted to individuals whose names appear on specific mailing lists. The nature of the mailing will match the interests of people on those lists. Many businesses are naturals for direct mail efforts. Magazine and book publishers have used mailings as their selling vehicle for many years, as have audiotape producers, clothing manufacturers, and shoe makers. Surprisingly, in the past few years there has been a growing list of high-priced goods sold in this manner, as well. Expensive paintings, numbered prints, sculptures, and collectibles are sold by mail these days.

But selling letters are not restricted to the mailings we receive daily in our mailboxes. Salespeople utilize business letters to sell their products or services, or to entice the buyer to accept a personal interview. Like the spoken presentation, the beginning of a business letter should grab the interest of the addressee, and tell him just enough—whetting his appetite to learn more.

Usually, letters loaded with statistical information, charts, and graphs are not effective, and mention of sales success with the addressee's competitors is more annoying than provocative. Instead, a letter with a straightforward, candid approach should be utilized, and heavy statistical matter omitted or sent as an enclosure.

Letters are used only when other means cannot be employed due to cost, distance, or time. They are no substitute for a personal call, yet they can be a powerful and effective sales tool. In the following pages, we will look at various kinds of letters designed to accomplish specific jobs.

The following letter was successful in securing an appointment, and ultimately a sale. Study the structure of the letter and adapt its form to fit your sales circumstance. Names, addresses, and locations have been changed.

◆   ◆   ◆

Mr. Robert Grey
Grey, Owens, and Pilcher
1212 Harbor Avenue
San Pedro, California 92655   7/9/92

Dear Mr. Grey:
Would you be surprised to learn that hand garden tools are the biggest profit centers in hardware stores all across America? Well, it's true!

Why should this interest Grey, Owens, and Pilcher? Because the rich rewards being harvested by hardware stores can be shared by you. In a pilot program here in Ohio, garden tools were introduced into such diverse outlets as supermarkets, drugstores, and convenience stores. Each has discovered that garden tools sell themselves when properly displayed and when adequate stock is available. Profit margins and stock turns are impressive.

Enclosed is more information and statistics that you will find of interest. Perhaps we can discuss this profitable opportunity further when I visit San Pedro early next month.

Green Thumb Tool Company,

John Riggs
Vice President/New Markets

◆   ◆   ◆

A letter like this tells the addressee only a little, but it isn't intended to do more. It is a teaser, aimed at getting the addressee eager to know more. It is low key and low pressure. It asks for nothing. The likely reaction to this is positive, and when the appointment is made, the seller can expect the prospect will have a high interest level. If the seller had made a personal call or a telephone call, it is unlikely the atmosphere would have been as receptive or open.

This next example sells a product. It is addressed to a buyer who cannot be reached through the normal channels.

◆   ◆   ◆

Mr. Thomas Hudkins   12/12/91
7875 Harper Boulevard
Dallas, Texas 77843

Dear Mr. Hudkins:

We were sorry to learn of your recent accident, but we are happy to know you are on your way to a complete recovery. I'm sure your doctor will advise you to continue with physical therapy at home and would endorse the use of the *Phys-aid* therapy machine.

In mishaps such as yours, the *Phys-aid* has proven to be an invaluable help in getting the patient back on his feet. Each *Phys-aid* machine is personally fitted to the patient, and a complete, personal introductory user program is also provided. The cost of *Phys-aid* is covered by most insurance programs.

Our therapy specialist, Rob Warren, will be in the Dallas area for two weeks beginning Monday, January 4,

1992, and he would be pleased to spend some time with you explaining the *Phys-aid* in detail, adapting it to your special needs, and teaching you how to get the most from this amazing machine.

Rob will telephone you early next week to arrange the appointment. Please have your insurance information available to facilitate billing. With best wishes, we remain,

Phys-aid, Incorporated

◆   ◆   ◆

The above letter is a strong, hard-selling letter. It tells the addressee what the product does and assumes the sale. "Please have your insurance information available" says "You just bought a Phys-aid machine." Notice that the letter doesn't tell much about the machine, except that it is important to recovery. If you were recuperating from an accident and knew that most insurance plans covered the cost of the machine, chances are you would be inclined to accept this solicitation.

Selling letters follow a regular sales presentation, although they are by necessity shorter and lighter, and the tease must be very strong. They close, but they must rely on the addressee to react to that close at a later time.

Many managers believe you must sell yourself before you can sell a product, but I don't agree with that. I've known highly successful salespeople who were not particularly liked by their customers. Still, you must sell yourself at some point in your career—especially when you are applying for or changing jobs. Following is a job-seeking letter sent to a company vice president. The applicant was a college student without work experience who had not been recommended or introduced to the employer. He had called the company, obtained the name of the marketing director, and was able to speak briefly with him. The marketing director (Griggs) invited the student to send in a resume (which was nothing more than a transcript of grades, and letters of recommendations from professors and employers). The applicant got the job and is doing well.

◆   ◆   ◆

Continental Merchandising Corp.   4/24/92
11987 North Kentucky Avenue
Chicago, Illinois 60711

Attention: John Griggs

Dear Mr. Griggs:

As you know, I am interested in becoming a member
of your marketing team, and I believe the enclosed resume with strengthen my claim for that job.

Before you review my resume, Mr. Griggs, allow me
to explain why I wish to join Continental. I have been
training for a career in marketing for the past four years
at State University, during which time I achieved A's in
all marketing-related courses. I researched the leading
merchandising companies to find those whose direction
and creativity would be compatible with mine. Only Continental and Acme Sales meet my standards.

At the risk of sounding like a first-class apple-
polisher, your reputation as a marketing man is a major
reason for my wanting to join Continental. Your volume
"Griggs Guide to Marketing," is a valued part of my personal library.

Allowing for mail delivery and your crowded calendar, I would imagine you will have had time to evaluate
my potential worth to CMC by the end of next week.
May I telephone you then to arrange a personal interview? Thank you.

Yours very truly,

Fred Akers
1777 No. Audabon Road
St. Louis, Missouri 25337
(314) 555-1212

◆ ◆ ◆

This letter shows an interested, studious applicant who has
done his homework about the company he wishes to join. Further, he shows he knows the accomplishments of the addressee.
His small compliment will be well received, you can be sure. If
you were an employer, wouldn't you want to know more about
such an applicant?

In earlier chapters we spoke of reviving a sale—doing

something to bring the buyer back to life. The following letter was received by a friend of mine after she had selected another candidate for a sales job. She was impressed and later hired the letter writer.

◆ ◆ ◆

Alexis Weathers   9/10/91
Harcourt and Wiseman
3765 Pope Street
San Francisco, CA 93302

Dear Ms. Weathers:
    I was disappointed, of course, to learn you had decided on another candidate for the sales position in Northern California. Nonetheless, I want to thank you for the time spent with me and for the fairness with which the interview was handled.
    As you know, I have been pointing towards a sales position with Harcourt and Wiseman for some time, and this setback will in no way diminish my interest in eventually becoming a part of your sales staff. With your permission I will stay in touch from time to time, and I hope you will consider me for some future position.
    It was a pleasure meeting you and getting to learn more about Harcourt and Wiseman. With sincere best wishes, I remain,

Yours truly,

John W. Wallace
Address/Telephone

◆ ◆ ◆

This thoughtful note was the only one of its kind ever received by Alexis, so you can imagine the impact it had. Not only does it show a determined job applicant, but it also suggests he would be a salesman who follows through in his territory.

Chapter 10

Person to Person

Sales is a numbers game. The more people you call, the more sales you make. If you mix in a fair amount of organization and planning, the calls produce even more sales. Add a dash of product knowledge, to a generous amount of skill, and you will find success in selling.

But not every call you make can produce a sale. Some buyers won't buy, others can't, some buyers become ill and aren't available. This is frustrating, annoying, and expensive. But it needn't be. Instead of reading a magazine or trading industry gossip with other salespeople, make your waiting time productive. If an appointment falls through, make the call productive anyway. How? By following a simple set of rules:

1. Review your post-call notes, and make certain you are prepared to follow up on those notes.
2. Take a careful inventory of your products to prepare your stock order.
3. Eyeball selling opportunities (look for holes in the inventory that you can fill and look at competitive products in stock that you can replace or compete with).
4. Sell the retail salespeople on the merits of your products.
5. Make sure point-of-sale material is available to the consumers.
6. If the buyer is available, review your sales presentation in preparation for your interview.
7. If you still have time, make telephone calls to your next account to firm up your next appointment.

No matter how important the buyer is, I make it a rule never to wait more than thirty minutes. You must always remember that the most important time you have is time spent with a decision maker. You must strive to spend as much time with him or her as possible, and although the thirty minutes you allow for waiting can be spent productively, it cannot conceivably replace the time spent with another buyer at your next stop. Maintain your dignity, and let the buyer know you are busy, and have no time to waste. He will get the message, and you will find that future visits will find him alert to the importance of your visit and the value of your time.

THE SALESPERSON YOU LEAVE BEHIND

The salesperson who sells to a retail store a product for resale must take special care to introduce himself to and make friends with the retail salesperson. These people are on the firing line every day, and they can have an enormous effect on the sell-through of your products. Most retail salespeople are thirsty for information and will be interested in what you can teach them. They are usually pretty knowledgeable, and you should not underestimate their abilities or intelligence. If you can sell them on the quality and utility of your product line, they will be your sales force to every consumer who shops there.

Retail salespeople are, however, often rigid and difficult to convince. Have patience, support your statements with outside facts verified by independent sources, provide samples, and in general treat them as you would the buyer. Many salespeople have a tendency to talk down to the retail salesperson, and that can be a disaster.

Take special care to be courteous and considerate. If a consumer is asking a question about your product, don't intrude on the sale. Try to catch the retail salesperson's eye, and indicate you'd like to help. In most cases they will be delighted—but they will very much appreciate your asking for permission.

The retail salesperson is particularly important to you if your line is a low-profile, seldom-advertised line. So much of today's retail sales are predetermined by massive advertising campaigns. We don't think about it, but when we visit the supermarket, for example, we automatically reach for particular brands because we are "programmed" to do so by advertising. We are sold by remote control.

You may have read about dramatic sales increases when this

or that product begins advertising on certain TV shows. The star of that show is given credit for the increase, and I will not quarrel with that. But the distribution, the merchandising, and the retail sales effort is usually overlooked. What if you advertised a new soft drink on the *Tonight Show*, but the consumer couldn't find the product in the store? Or what if the sales merchandiser put the product in the most obscure place in the store or sold against it? Sales would lag.

The retail sales effort can have a tremendous effect. I know of a national chain that allows its salespeople spiffs. (Spiffs are small retail bonuses paid for each retail sale of a particular product.) In that chain, I have seen product with extensive advertising campaigns supporting them sitting untouched on the shelves, while spiffed product flew out the door. If you want your product to sell through in that chain, there is only one way to do it—reward the salesperson.

GESTURES AND BODY LANGUAGE

Most of us notice body language and gestures, and we understand them. When a buyer folds his arms across his chest, we should be wary, since he may be telling us he is closed to our ideas. Crossing the arms is also a gesture of disgust and is often accompanied by a look of disdain or doubt. Someone who crosses his legs and swings his foot back and forth is telling us he is in a hurry. Drumming fingers on a desk or frequent glances at a wristwatch speak loudly. Cupping hands behind the head tells us the person is relaxed and willing to listen. Watch for other telltale signs, and be alert to the gestures and hand signals of the buyer; they can help you in selecting the tactic you use in selling your prospect.

For the salesperson, gestures and hand signals are not only useful, they must be used in every presentation. For example, *when it is time* to show your product, show it with a flair. Don't simply take it from your sales case and hand it to the buyer; instead showcase it. Cradle it in your hands gently as if it were a precious commodity.

Similarly, a shrug of the shoulders, the slightest shaking of the head or narrowing of the brows, can convey that you question the claims of a competitor without making you an envious attacker.

When you use gestures in your sales presentation, it eliminates or reduces inhibition, it makes you feel exuberant, it heightens excitement and draws the prospect into the spirit of your presentation. Many buyers are, by nature, reserved people. They talk quietly, and their conversations are devoid of gestures. When they are exposed to an exciting, gesture-filled presentation, they not only react positively to it, they are thrilled by it! It's fun for them, they remember you and your product, and the memory is associated with a pleasant experience.

Gestures and Emotion

Remember, virtually all sales are made by touching some emotion in the buyer. A salesperson will always use hand signals and body language when showing a car. He will sweep his hand across the hood to indicate the power within. When he invites you to sit in the car, he will do so with hand gestures.

Real-estate agents will use gestures similar to the automobile salesperson when showing a house. They will sweep their hands in a widening gesture when they show the closet space. I had one salesman stretch to his full height as he showed how our Christmas tree would fit in the bay window!

Commercial television and advertising agencies know all this, of course, and their messages are cloaked in emotion-provoking gestures. The beautiful young girl who lowers her sunglasses to watch the sleek, red Corvette whiz by speaks volumes about what the Corvette will supposedly do for your social life, and it sells many automobiles. The handsome, sun-bronzed surfers at the beach stop to stare, mouths agape at that one special sunbather in a Catalina swimsuit.

All of these gestures, body language, and looks appeal to the emotions of the buyer. You must incorporate gestures into your sales presentation if you wish to add a dash of excitement and get the most out of every selling opportunity.

One word of caution: be careful not to overdo gestures. You can detract from your presentation and rob yourself of the buyer's attention with gestures that are too flamboyant. Naturally, all gestures should add to your presentation, and should never be vulgar or offensive.

Chapter 11

Words That Sell

In this chapter we will look at twelve power words. These are words that according to researchers are the most pleasing words to the American ear. Tested against hundreds of other words, these were highly rated words, best able to change the attitudes of the listener. There are, of course, more than a dozen words in our language that persuade and convince, but these are the most powerful.

◆ ◆ ◆

What you say and how you say it is important. I believe that closing should start early and should be included in every part of the sale. So we should aim at closing the sale from the very beginning. The selection of the words we use throughout the sale are, therefore, crucial.

"Ms. Jenkins, we have found the answer to
acne with Blemish Begone."

"Ms. Jenkins, our discovery, Blemish Begone,
has banished acne forever."

Can you detect the power word in either of those two statements? The power word is *discovery*. What is it about this word that makes it powerful? *Discovery* suggests a breakthrough, a fresh, new, heretofore unknown something has been uncovered. The word is linked with adventure and exploration. The discovery of America, the discovery of Dr. Livingston—these are thrilling, exciting, new, and different things.

"Mr. Ford, an easy and proven method to
improve your game is explained in this book."

"Mr. Ford, a positive way to improve your
game is explained in this book."

Both statements say the same thing and both are perfectly fine. However, one statement is the more powerful—one will sell more often than the other. In these examples, two power words are used. Can you detect them? The two words are *easy* and *proven*. Americans are well known for not wanting things too complicated. Japanese camera makers could never understand why American families had less than one 35mm camera per family, whereas the Japanese family averaged more than four per family. The answer was simple: Americans didn't enjoy complicated F stops, lens speed, and composition, all required to obtain good photographs. When the Japanese introduced the easy-to-operate point-and-shoot cameras, sales shot up. To operate these cameras all one needed to do was aim and click. The camera did the rest.

Proven is a guarantee. *Proven* means (in the minds of buyers) tested and guaranteed. It also suggests that the product or service has been judged against other competing products or services.

"This washer-dryer will cut your wash day in
half."

"This washer-dryer will save you an entire
morning."

Once again we have two power words in one of the above examples. Which are they? The words are *save* and *you*. Saving money, or time, or grief, or trouble—these are all things we like to do in our lives. So if this washer-dryer will save us an entire morning, it is something we relate to immediately. This is subtle, perhaps, but it lies in our subconscious. We all want to save. *You* personalizes. If the statement were "This washer-dryer will save the average homemaker an entire morning," it would depersonalize and separate the product from the person to which it is aimed. When reading an advertisement, people ask themselves how it will benefit them. Even the thoughtful husband, who wants to surprise his wife with a labor-saving device, considers how that appliance will benefit *him*. Will *his* life be made easier? Will the new units be quiet so *he* can watch the TV undisturbed? And, incidentally, will it make things easier for her, too? Thus, the experts tell us, goes the thinking, although these days a wife is probably just as likely to buy a washer for her husband.

> "This outboard is one of our finest and carries
> a full year guarantee."

> "This outboard is one of our finest and has an
> excellent record for durability."

Pretty obvious that time, huh? The power word is *guarantee*. We all grew up with the idea that a guarantee was a promise, an unbreakable pledge. Hence, we react favorably to the word. During a sales presentation, you might say, "I guarantee this will be one of your customer's favorite products." In actuality, you are probably not guaranteeing anything of consequence, but the very use of the word carries perceptions that a promise is being made.

> "Investing in this CD will return a handsome
> 6.7% in annual interest."

> "Investing in this CD will return a healthy
> 6.7% in annual interest."

Once again we are talking about perception. The customer reacts to words that convey good things happening. *Healthy* is the operative word here. The most important thing in our material life is our health and the health of those we care about. You will often see the word *healthy* used in advertising everything from lifestyles to alarm systems.

> "Protect your money, but more important,
> protect those you love, with a Gottcha home
> alarm system."

> "Protect yourself and your family with
> Gottcha home alarm systems."

The word is *you* (and its cousin *your*). Willie Sutton, the famous bank robber, wrote that when threatening someone, you should always direct your threat at a specific part of the body. Never say, "Do what I say or I'll shoot you." Instead, say, "Do what I say or I'll blow your kneecaps off." Willie knew his trade, and probably would have been a good salesman. When you direct someone's attention to a specific body part, he sees things in a very personal way. (No, I *don't* advise using Willie's presentation-at-gunpoint technique with tough buyers!)

I was informed about a recent sales situation in which the buyer was a woman in her forties. The salesperson was selling a product that helped to correct memory loss. The presentation was going poorly, until the salesperson asked the buyer, "Do you have a mother or grandmother, someone *you love* who is suffering forgetfulness? You know, can't recall where she left her keys, forgets appointments, that sort of thing?" Immediately the buyer started to show interest. "Why yes," she answered. "My favorite aunt is worried about this. With all the talk about Alzheimer's, the poor dear is frantic. She tries to hide her forgetfulness, and that just makes it worse." Perhaps the salesperson would have made the sale anyway, but by personalizing and asking if the buyer knew of someone she loved, she used two power words, personalized the sale, and got the order plus an in-store promotion.

✦ ✦ ✦

We are all familiar with new and improved products that come on the market. We have all probably made an appointment by telling the buyer we had a new idea or new product he just had to see. *New* is a strong selling word because the world is built on change. People are rarely satisfied with the status quo. They want new things, new ideas, new challenges, and new opportunities. Newness drives us forward, makes us reach, and as Americans we like to stretch as far as we can.

"*You* will *love* the *proven results* of the *new* Wombat computer, the *easy*-to-operate, user-friendly computer that will *guarantee* your *safety* from computer viruses." This statement is loaded with power words. The new ones are *results* and *safety*.

Results is what we are after. As your boss has probably told you a few hundred times by now, "I want results." What are the results of the third race at Santa Anita or the Mets twilight doubleheader, or the Monday night Miami Dolphins game? Results give us answers—positive answers, and that's good. At the same time, we want *safety*. The car we drive must deliver us to our destination safely. Volvo has successfully sold this feature on the safety record of its automobiles.

So there you have it: the twelve most powerful, convincing, closing words in the English language. Remember them, and weave them into your presentation:

discovery	love	results
easy	money	safety
guarantee	new	save
healthy	proven	you

Earlier, we talked about the power of asking questions as you go along in your sales presentations. Pacing is important when you ask questions—and when you wait for answers. I've seen many a sale lost because the salesperson talked too soon or was too anxious to use his closing technique. He saw that he had boxed the buyer in and wanted to go for the kill.

The auto salesman is told, "We want to think it over. We just don't make decisions involving that much money quickly." When hit with "we want to think it over," stall. Review what has transpired: "Folks, when someone tells me they want to think it over, I'm sure I've failed to give them all the information they need to make a decision. Now perhaps this car isn't what you want. What is it about the car you don't like?"

"Do you think it is underpowered?" (No, it is a great engine.) "The Mrs. seemed to like the interior." (Oh, I love it.) "The gas mileage is outstanding." (We are impressed with that, especially.) "Well, now, let me think, you love the looks, the handling, the mechanics, the safety and the economy of the car—what else could it be?"

"Oh, we love the car, it's just that we want to sleep on the decision."

"It could only be one thing. Money. Don't think you can afford it?"

"Well, we want to review our situation."

"Folks, if I could sell you this car tonight for $5,000 less than the price I quoted you, could you afford to buy it?"

"Of course, but I don't think you can sell it for $5,000 less than the quote."

"You're right. But $5,000 is what is coming between owning this beautiful car and driving your old car home. So we are really talking about $5,000, aren't we?"

"I guess we are."

"How long do you normally keep a car? Five years?"

"Oh we trade in about every seven years."

"OK, but let's assume you trade in five years—I'll give you the benefit of the doubt. Do you sometimes stop for a cup of coffee and a donut in the morning on your way to work?"

"Why, yes, but not just for coffee, I usually have breakfast in a shop near my home."

"Would you say you average $2.75 a day for your breakfast?"

"More than that, probably about $5.00 a day."

"Sir, you can own this car for less than $2.75 per day."

"What? I don't follow you."

(*Explain that $2.75 per day X 365 days per year X 5 years = $5,018.75.*)

"So if you can manage to eliminate your coffee shop breakfast, cigarettes, movies, or any number of tiny things we all spend money on, the car is yours—tonight. Can you make that adjustment?"

"Well, when you break it down, yes, I guess I can do it. Write up the deal."

The foregoing is known as breaking down the deal to the smallest denominator. Once the prospect sees that it is just $2.75 per day, he thinks, "Heck, I can save $2.75 per day. He is no longer struggling with handling a $24,000 automobile. Instead, he is grappling with just $2.75 per day—he spends more than that on breakfast! Can you see how this works for the salesperson?

But none of it would work if the salesperson jumps to a conclusion about what was holding up the sale. If the salesperson had, say, tried to trade them down, they would not have bought. If he had squeezed them for more money immediately, they would have proclaimed they wanted to think it over. Instead, the salesperson walked them through the presentation again. "You like this, you loved that, you agreed to this—so what's not to like?"

This sale came about because the salesperson was patient, he listened, he reviewed, and he was prepared. Early on he asked: "If I could sell you this car for $5,000 less than the quoted price, could you afford it?" That is a qualifier and a close. Yes we could afford it *(and we can safely assume they would buy it for a $5,000 discount)*. So now his only problem is proving to them that they can afford it. Breaking things down to daily cost simplifies things and lets the buyer work with figures that he can handle in his head.

One last thing to be noted. The salesperson *gave* something. When the prospect was asked how long he normally drove his car, he answered seven years—the salesperson gave him two years. This allows the salesperson an easier figure to work with in his arithmetic, and it lets the customer say to himself, "if it only costs $2.75 per day for five years—it'll cost even less if I keep the car seven years."

Little things can affect a sale. Your choice of words will affect your prospect's decision; sharp and descriptive words personalize a sale. And a major sale can be clinched when the salesperson reduces the cost to a daily amount.

Chapter 12

Promoting Sales

Retailers (especially the tough buyers!) who are unsuccessful in selling their wares try to return unsold goods. This causes all sorts of problems for the buyer and the seller, not the least of which are charge-backs on the commission statement.

Buyers dislike taking markdowns, since it affects the bottom line of their department's profit-and-loss statement. This affects bonus payments the buyer might make, which in turn affects the bonus the merchandise manager can make. If a category experiences too many product markdowns, heads will roll.

The salesperson the buyer loves to see is the salesperson whose goods sell out of the store. A retail operation today is a highly competitive arena, and what is available in one store is usually available in any number of others. Trying to be different is a daily struggle, and trying to offer the consumer reasons to shop in his store is the pre-eminent goal of today's buyer. But how does the buyer accomplish this?

Buyers are desperate for new ideas and new methods to sell merchandise. They seek vendors who can create fresh, exciting promotions that will attract shoppers and sell goods. Without promotions, a retail store becomes dull and boring, the store cannot attract new customers, and old customers are lured away.

◆ ◆ ◆

The wise salesperson will conceive of product promotions that snag the new customer, hold on to the old customer, accelerate the sale of goods, and help to educate and inspire retail salespeople.

Obviously, the most common promotional practice is cutting prices. A sale to many buyers simply means slashing profit margins. The buyer often expects a portion of the lost profits to be absorbed by the vendor. It isn't fair, but if you're creative enough, it needn't be the case. The salesperson who can devise a promotion that avoids deep price cuts will find a warm welcome waiting for him in most buying offices.

Promotions cost money, and retailers are normally tight-fisted. Yet there are ways to create the funds to run elaborate promotions. (Always bear in mind that a promotion must pay for itself.)

Almost every product has a slush price—money that can be taken out of the price charged in the form of discounts, or money that can be used for promotion and advertising. For example: suppose you are selling ice skates to sporting goods stores. An important customer is a twenty-store chain who stocks your skates along with five other brands. You want to promote the sale of your product, but your company has no advertising budget. What do you do?

First of all, determine the amount of slush monies available. Explain to your sales manager the promotion you have in mind, and ask if any additional monies might be made available (usually not, but it doesn't hurt to try). Let's assume the skates cost $40 per pair wholesale, and there is $6 per pair in slush money.

Second, think of an innovative method to promote the sale of your skates; something that will attract customers. Let's say you are interested in gaining the preteen shopper. Think—what do most preteens enjoy? Answer: cassette tapes. Most tapes cost $7 each (on average), and you are going to give away as prizes 200 of the most popular cassettes.

Third, you contact a large retail chain or distributor of cassette tapes. Explain to the general manager or the sales manager what you are planning on doing. Show them how they will benefit by taking part in your promotion. (The company name prominently displayed in twenty sporting goods stores; exposure to hundreds of preteen buyers.)

Perhaps they will donate the tapes at no cost to you or allow a generous discount. Suppose they sell you the tapes at $4 each. This means you will have $2 to use for advertising, printing, and miscellaneous expenses.

Fourth, you contact the buyer and explain the promotion: In each of his stores there will be a stack display of your ice skates. A header card will invite the preteen customer and anyone else to enter the contest. (Since music tapes are the prizes, this will attract most attention from preteens.) Entry forms will be made available at the display and at all checkout counters. To enter the contest, the customer fills out an entry blank and sends this along with an end-panel from the skate box (or a replica thereof) to your offices. Two hundred names will then be drawn at random and the tapes will be sent to them.

This is what a promotion like this can accomplish:

1. For the contest period your skates will be prominently displayed, featured, and sold.
2. Your skates will outsell the competition during the sales period, and perhaps beyond.
3. New customers will be attracted to the store, gaining goodwill from the buyer and store managers.
4. The buyer will have to stock more skates than normal to cover himself for the expected sales increase.
5. If the promotion is successful, the retail salespeople will have become familiar with your skates and will probably continue to sell your brand long after the promotion is over.
6. The buyer will remember you as an innovative and thoughtful salesperson. They will come to you for other promotional ideas, and they will favor you over the competition.

Department stores, large discount stores, and others will sometimes be so anxious to have a sales promotion that they will ask you to overbill on merchandise, the excessive billing being returned to them in the form of advertising monies. For instance, suppose your ice skates are sold in a department store chain. The wholesale price has been pared to the point where no slush money is available, yet the buyer wants the promotion you outlined for him. In a case like this, he may ask you to bill him at $45 per pair ($5 over the normal cost); the extra $5 will be rebated to the store for promotional expense.

Why would a buyer do such a thing, since the money is coming out of his company's pockets? Because it is the only way to get open-to-buy money available to him, to help him promote the merchandise. He reasons that the goods will sell through, and that the profit will easily offset the money he has extracted from his open-to-buy.

As mentioned in earlier chapters, retail salespeople can be powerful allies in the retail wars that rage daily in America's stores. The salesperson spends an hour or two with the buyer, and the power and energy of your presentation stays with him. The people charged with the responsibility of selling your merchandise are too often ignored. This can be a serious mistake. Believe me, it pays to endear yourself and your products to the retail sales staff.

One of the simplest ways of doing this is by arranging a spiff program. As we noted earlier, the spiff is a small cash bonus given to a retail salesperson for each designated unit sold.

To carry the example of the ice skate promotion a step further, suppose you have $1,440 to use in your promotion. You spend $1,000 for the prizes, and have $440 left to use in any way you wish. Instead of buying additional tapes to be given away to the consumer, which will probably not add anything to the promotion, it would be smart to pay a $2 spiff to the retail salespeople for the first 220 pairs sold. This encourages the retail salespeople to get involved in the promotion, to push it at store-level, and to hustle for the spiff money. This naturally delights the store manager and the department manager, since they can see their people excited and interested in the promotion. The buyer is pleased since it almost ensures a sell-out, and it should please the salesperson, especially when commissions are figured.

Remember that retail salespeople are normally not paid a great deal. Their salaries are minimal and an opportunity to earn an extra $20 is welcomed. I have known some extraordinary sales talents who work retail, and some earn as much as $4,000 or more in spiff money every month. How would you like to have a salesperson who can earn that kind of bonus working for you after you leave the account?

THE MYSTERY SHOPPER

One of the wholesale salesperson's biggest problems is getting the retailer to offer his goods first to the consumer. If one could accomplish this, he could probably go to the head of the class very quickly. But retailers, like all of us, have their favorite products and favorite salespeople, so they sell what they want to sell, rather than what their bosses want them to sell. Spiffs can change that in your favor very quickly. However, not all stores allow them, feeling that they make their people too pushy. Ask your buyer for his company's policy concerning spiffs, and if they are not allowed, don't despair: there are other ways to achieve the same results.

Some years ago, the marketing manager of a national brewery, ranked third in the nation in sales, came up with an idea that catapulted his company into first place almost overnight. His company had good distribution, had won taste awards, and advertised just as much as the competition. But beer drinkers, it was believed, were loyal to their brands, and getting them to switch was a difficult, almost impossible, task. But the marketing manager was determined to try.

After testing various ideas, the sales manager noticed some interesting facts. Many customers have no brand loyalty at all. When they visited a favorite tavern, the would order simply by saying, "Gimme a beer." No brand was mentioned. He further noticed that the bartenders rarely reached for XYZ beer, each bartender having his favorite. That was a key point, getting the *bartender* to reach for XYZ brand when the customer said, "Gimme a beer."

The marketing team struggled with the problem for weeks. Finally the marketing manager got a very bright idea. He hired a number of people to act as customers who would visit key cafes, restaurants, and bars in a test market area. They would order a beer at each stop they made. If the bartender served them XYZ brand, they would hand him a $5 bill along with a note that read: "I am the XYZ brewery mystery shopper. This $5 bill is your reward for serving me XYZ beer when I ordered a beer. Keep it up. I, or another mystery shopper, may be back at any time."

On the other hand, if the bartender served a competing brand, the mystery shopper would pay for the brew and hand the bartender a card that read: "I am the XYZ mystery shopper. If you had served me an XYZ beer when I ordered, I would have rewarded you with a $5 tip. Sorry! But you will have another chance; a mystery shopper may stop at your bar at any time. Be sure to serve XYZ when someone says, 'I'll have a beer.' You never know, it could be the mystery shopper."

It was a brilliant marketing idea—and it worked. Naturally, the bartenders had nothing to lose by serving XYZ beer if the customer didn't specify the brand. Sales skyrocketed.

Take Me to ...

An Italian restaurant in St. Louis conceived of a similar promotion. It was doing a fair neighborhood business and that, the owner/manager believed, was a potential problem. Neighborhoods never stay the same. This was an Italian-American neighborhood but the ethnic mix could change. Many of the people in the neighborhood were tradesmen and blue-collar workers whose incomes were tied to the construction industry. Good weather usually meant steady paychecks. Rain and cold meant economic difficulties. The restaurant owner could see his sales following the economic and social conditions of the neighborhood.

Not very far away was a cluster of quality hotels filled with prosperous businessmen, visiting sports professionals, and tourists. If he could only reach that market, his restaurant would be assured a steady stream of business. But how could he reach these people? He tried newspaper advertising without measurable results. He placed half-page ads in the yellow pages of the telephone book and saw his business continue at a rather predictable pace.

Then, one snowy evening as he sat in his office, which overlooked the main entrance, he saw a taxi pull up to the door, and a load of wealthy diners pile out. "Taxis," he mused. "Most business travelers and others staying at those fancy hotels take taxi cabs to dinner, and usually they ask the cab driver for a restaurant recommendation." In that instant, he had the solution to his problem.

First, the owner renovated the basement of his restaurant and set up an attractive, comfortable dining room. The atmosphere was warm and friendly and the food was the very same as that served in the dining room above. He then contacted every taxi company in St. Louis and posted on the drivers' bulletin board an offer of a free meal for every ten customers delivered to his door. When a cab driver delivered a diner, he received a chit for every passenger.

Soon the restaurant was packed, upstairs and down. It has become nationally famous and is a favorite hangout for sports figures, businessmen, politicians, and visiting celebrities. Tourists and business travelers spread the word all across the nation: when you visit St. Louis, you must eat at this restaurant. The promotion was so successful that within two years a large addition was needed. The owner/manager continues this promotion to this day, and the restaurant continues to prosper.

Chapter 13

"My Buddy"

Business contact, especially between the salesperson and the buyer, often includes entertainment: dinners, sporting events, plays, even home entertainment. There is nothing wrong with entertaining or becoming friends with customers, but there is a fine line that you must walk, because becoming too chummy with a customer carries risks for both parties.

I believe it is the wisest course to entertain business friends at company functions. Golf tournaments, the company Christmas party, the summer picnic, a group night at the ballpark, and similar activities can bring the customer closer to the company, give him a feeling of association, let him meet others he talks with and depends on, and, at the same time, maintain that barrier that keeps the business relationship distinct from a personal one.

During a business week you may find it expedient to invite your customer to lunch. Business lunches should be just that—an opportunity to get away from telephones and other distractions, enjoy a fine lunch, and discuss business in a relaxed atmosphere. Tickets to plays, concerts, and sporting events are acceptable ways of saying thank you, but they should not be used to buy orders.

If the salesperson accompanies the buyer to any of these events, dinner is usually part of the evening. This is OK, but drinking should be carefully restricted.

The formality of a business office is useful for both parties. When formality is eliminated, when the salesperson becomes chummy with the buyer, the relationship changes, usually for the worse. The salesperson begins to take the buyer for granted. Instead of working for the orders and doing the best he can to secure them, the salesperson assumes his old buddy will take care of him. In short, he depends on his personal relationship instead of his sales prowess and the value of his merchandise.

A buyer may feel ashamed of his behavior when he lets his hair down. This can result in avoiding the salesperson. Sometimes the buyer will make demands that exceed the salesperson's expense account and exceeds the value of the account itself. If that happens, the salesperson is put in an awkward situation; if he tells the buyer he cannot grant his wish, the buyer will be offended. On the other hand, if he grants his wish, the salesman feels he has been taken advantage of, and he will resent that. As a result, the salesman might start making demands of his own and a vicious circle begins.

In a business relationship, the salesperson is totally at ease if he must push for a bigger order, a better merchandise situation, or whatever. It's his job. The buyer, should he decide the offer isn't in the best interest of his company, is comfortable when he refuses the offer. When friendship is inserted, neither buyer nor seller is free to do his job in the best way.

Friendship can render the salesperson frustrated and helpless. If he pushes for more business, which is his job, the buyer feels compromised. If he doesn't push, the salesperson feels weakened. The buyer will resent being forced to make a decision that he cannot justify to his boss, or he may find he must defend his friendship with the salesperson.

If an overstock develops, the buyer may assume his friend will arrange for a return. If that isn't granted, he may feel the salesperson is taking advantage of their friendship, while at the same time the salesperson may feel the buyer is making demands he wouldn't make of others.

THE GUY DOWN THE BLOCK

It is only natural for friends to help friends. During a conversation, a buyer could mention he needs a big profit month. The salesperson will try to give his friend a special deal, a lower price, sell him the best product he has, or grant some other favor at the expense of all his other customers. These kinds of favors can't be secrets; they always get out. The guy down the block hears about the special deal his competitor is getting and demands the same deal. The salesperson can't grant these favors to everyone, and he ends up losing customers. Even if the salesperson isn't granting special favors, the competition will be inclined to believe so.

Let's say you know a buyer who is friendly with a competitor of yours. You resent the fact that your competitor can visit the buyer at any time he chooses. They play golf, go to the races, attend baseball games, and entertain in each other's homes. You see the competitor's goods stacked up in the stores, and you can't help but resent it.

Nevertheless, you should never attempt to compete with that sort of situation by trying to develop a friendship of your own. Instead, do your job in a professional way, learn all you can about the needs of your customer, then see how your product can relate to those needs. Serve the customer after the sale (so few salespeople do that), always be fair and honest, and you'll be rewarded and respected. And you will not have to suffer all the risks that business friendships entail.

Use these ten points to compete with the salesperson who is everyone's buddy.

1. Find a need your customer has. He may not know he has that need or he may not be able to define it, so you'll have to study his business and prove to him how your product will help his business, how your product will fill that need.
2. Remember the mechanics of selling and never stray from those four rules.
3. Develop a dialogue with the buyer, and get him involved in the sale; the more he talks, the more you learn. Talking buyers never walk.
4. Always ask questions that assist the dialogue and draw out information from the buyer. Then ask questions that close.
5. Learn to listen. The buyer may be trying to tell you what he wants.
6. Always close—as early as practical—and as often as necessary.
7. Remember: if the buyer says no he may be saying, "Convince me."
8. When they say OK, write the order and leave.
9. Close after the close.
10. Always follow up and fulfill every promise you make.

THE JOKE IS ON YOU

A master salesman once gave me a great tip: "One of the things I try to teach my salespeople is always make certain your jokes are in good taste. Never tell an ethnic joke, a joke about any religion, or one about a particular political party."

This is good advice. Of course, telling an ethnic joke might easily offend. So too might jokes relating to religion or politics. Sexist jokes are frowned on as well. I make it a practice to tell jokes only if they fit into the presentation in some way, if they are on me, or if I can be absolutely certain no offense can be taken. Lately, I find that discovering jokes that don't offend *someone* is becoming harder and harder! But I still take care.

Chapter 14

Personality and Appearance

Not everyone has a winning personality nor is everyone instantly likable. However, most people can be liked if we give them a chance. If we take the time to see what makes someone tick, we can usually discover something to admire.

Unfortunately, in business and especially in selling, we don't always have a lot of time to make an impression, and many times the buyer will not take the trouble to discover we are likable. So it is up to the salesperson to develop a personality that will allow him to play on an even field with the competition.

Personality is composed of a number of things, and the most important component is attitude. Your attitude says so much about you: about how you approach your job, whether you are truly interested in the problems your customer has, whether you are dependable, honest, and fair. Many managers feel that attitude—some call it enthusiasm—is the most important characteristic a salesperson should have, and a lot of people agree with them.

What develops a good attitude more than anything else is belief in what your company is doing and knowing the benefits the products you sell provide. Understanding these things and believing in them will give you self-confidence, which will carry over to every sales situation. When you are so enthusiastic you can't wait to get to your next call, the days fly by, and getting business seems so easy you almost feel guilty when payday comes.

The attitude and enthusiasm you have toward your work will be reflected in the attitude you have toward your job, your customer, and in every fiber of your life. Work becomes fun, you will be excited about sharing your knowledge with the buyer, delighted to show him how he can benefit by using your merchandise or service, and eager to cross swords with him when he questions or compares.

Learning about your product or service, really learning about it—every facet, every strength, and every weakness—develops self-confidence and self-confidence develops positive, energy-bursting enthusiasm. It will carry you a long way.

◆ ◆ ◆

There is a saying, "You only get one chance to make a first impression." This is true, and because it's true, the wise salesperson will take care about his personal appearance. The way you dress can have an important affect on the buyer's opinion of you and your company. I've heard buyers say, "The guy had scuffed shoes, unpressed trousers—I mean, he was a mess. If he doesn't care about himself, is he going to care about my business?"

You may be just starting in sales and not have a lot of money for a wardrobe. Take my advice: go to a good specialty store, give yourself over to the owner or a salesperson who has worked there for years, and tell them what you want to accomplish. They'll show you how a necktie and a pocket handkerchief or a colorful blouse can change your entire appearance; they'll suggest colors that flatter you, and they'll keep a watch on your budget, too. As you progress in your work, add to your wardrobe. It can make the buyer see you in a positive light, and even more important, it can make you see yourself in a more positive way. Part of self-confidence is personal appearance.

Since Americans are, perhaps, the most fastidious people in the world, I'm almost embarrassed to mention personal grooming. Our awareness of attention to personal grooming is aided by the massive advertising campaigns we are subjected to every day. Ads for shaving creams, toothpaste, mouthwash, lipstick, and cosmetics of all kinds keep reminding us to be vigilant in personal grooming. Still, we can get busy and forget that we need a haircut or a manicure. These are small things, but important for our own self-image as well as the image we project to others.

Personal mannerisms and annoying habits may be devastating to a salesperson. Tugging your ear, rubbing your nose, scratching your head, and other mannerisms can be annoying and distracting to strangers. Most people are unaware they are doing the things that annoy and distract, and even close friends or family, so used to the habits, may pay no attention.

Practicing your presentation before a mirror is a help. You may be surprised at the lack of gestures or the emergence of a mannerism that takes away from your presentation. Buyers have confided in me that this salesperson or that drives them nuts, because he fidgets, crosses and uncrosses his legs, or fiddles with his tie. Mannerisms are one of those small areas that can have a large affect on your sales acceptance.

✦ ✦ ✦

The sales personality is a combination of attitude, knowledge, appearance, mannerisms, and ambition. Yes, ambition. To be a winner, you have to want to win. You've heard sports announcers say: "This or that team *wanted the victory* more than the other." Analyze yourself. Determine what you really want from your job. Do you really want to be a success at sales? Do you know what you want from each and every call you make? You may be surprised at the answers. Winning at anything involves tradeoffs and sacrifice. If someone chooses to be a professional athlete, he knows he must train hard, travel constantly, maintain a rigorous, special diet, and give every performance 100 percent. He must want that life very much to sacrifice so many things. Business isn't much different. If you really want success, you have to plan and practice, work and sacrifice.

I stress the need to plan and to know exactly what you want from every call you make. I've seen many salespeople fail to get the order because they didn't know what they wanted to sell! I know that sounds foolish, but it is true. I've worked with salespeople who chatted about sports, hobbies, and everything else on their way to a call. In the parking lot, they might mention some characteristic of the buyer: "This guy is a stickler on quality," or some such remark.

"What are you going to sell this buyer?" I would ask.

The salesperson would come back with the same reply—"Whatever I can." This would drive me to distraction and remind me of the salesperson who starts his interview with the remark, "I was just in the neighborhood and . . . ." The buyer is too important and much too busy to have you drop by because you were just in the neighborhood! One should always stress that the interview is important and should be planned for carefully. You will be impressed with the change in the buyer's attitude toward you.

Taking targets of opportunity may become necessary due to some unforeseen occurrence—but the salesperson who knows precisely what he wants to sell is better prepared, more knowledgeable, and more enthusiastic. When you have focus, you will naturally prepare for the call. You will gather together all the support materials you require and will review the strengths and weaknesses of your product or service. You will rehearse your presentation and be ready for any questions or rebuttal. Being prepared gives you enthusiasm, self-confidence, and an eagerness to sell.

SQUARE PEGS AND ROUND HOLES

A common mistake many salespeople make is trying to sell merchandise or services that have no relevance to the buyer's business. If you were selling shoes, you would be careful to measure for proper size before showing various styles. But in other kinds of sales it may not be so easy to determine exactly what your customer needs. Some salespeople start talking before they have the faintest idea what this particular customer may need. This is why asking questions is crucial.

Before one even makes an appointment with the buyer, one should investigate and learn as much about the account as he can. Learn what products are presently stocked, or what companies supply them. Understand the markets they are shooting for and the strategy they use. For example, a mass market superstore may be more concerned with national brand names than with unique, stylish merchandise. A specialty store will be more interested in products that are not readily available, and price may not be a major consideration.

There are trends in merchandising that will determine what will be stocked and sold. A few years ago price was the most important merchandising factor with national retail chains. Recently, major retailers have swung toward better quality goods, or at least brand-name goods. Keeping an eye on these trends will help you make your presentation timely and intelligent.

When you try to fit square pegs into round holes, you waste the buyer's time and he marks you in that way. You will find it difficult to get appointments, since he believes you have nothing of interest for him, and when you do get an appointment, his attitude will be negative. This isn't to discourage opening new markets for products. The buyer may say, "We don't sell garden tools; I don't have any interest in doing so." But he may not realize how many other stores like his already carry garden tools and do a great job with them. Now you see, I hope, why knowing what you want to sell and knowing what your prospect's goals are are so important.

Being prepared and planning your call allows you to control the interview. You will be able to direct the presentation and aim the buyer toward the closing question. He becomes a part of the process instead of being an adversary. When he sees benefits he will ask more probing questions, and when you have the answers, you will also have the sale.

Even if he doesn't buy immediately, he will be interested in seeing you again. You will be known as a professional, someone who will contribute to his business.

We've talked about using gestures and body language in selling. It is also important to use printed selling aids. People remember what they see longer and more clearly than what they hear. The expression "A picture is worth a thousand words" is proven over and over in sales presentations. This is particularly true when outside support materials are available. (Outside support materials are newspaper and magazine articles, industry publications, and similar props that strengthen your sale.)

Having working samples available for the buyer is likewise of great value. I know sales professionals who insist on getting the buyer to hold the sample in his hands. According to these pros, it transfers ownership and gives the buyer a psychological attachment to the product. It works.

Not long ago, a salesman told me about his problems in trying to sell children's vitamins to a national chain. His product was good, but so was the competition's. No matter what tack he took, the competition was just as good. He could see the buyer was wrapping up the interview.

The salesman had done his homework, he had carefully researched children's vitamins, and believed the most important feature was taste. All competitive products had basically the same formula, but each had a distinctive flavor. He had kids of his own, and by having them and their friends taste various flavors, he discovered that flavors such as pineapple, raspberry, and apple were not popular.

Only one flavor seemed popular with all—strawberry. Visiting a college library, he discovered that his belief had been the subject of a research paper that drew an identical conclusion. "Mr. Buyer, our vitamins for kids taste like fresh strawberries—here, taste one," he urged.

The buyer tasted the vitamin and agreed it did, indeed, taste like fresh strawberries. "But, so what? I like the tart apple that Nature's Finest has," he said.

"Respectfully, Mr. Buyer, I don't want to sell *you* the children's vitamins, I want to sell them to the kids. They take vitamins at their parent's insistence, but if they don't like the taste, the parents switch again and again. Now I've tried the strawberry-flavored vitamins on my own children and their friends. They all love strawberry."

"Yeah?" answered the buyer. "My kids like the apple."

The salesman smiled and shook his head in a knowing way, "Well, you just never know, but I went to the library and researched children's preference for various flavors—strawberry won hands down. Here is the paper; read it for yourself."

You can imagine the force and power this paper had—a university research paper supporting the salesman's closing point. The sale was made. This is an excellent example of what planning and focus can do for you.

Support materials are particularly important when making presentations to buyers who must carry your message to a committee. The buyer you speak to cannot possibly recall all the positive points of your presentation. He has dozens of products to present and will usually have a few notes and his own impressions that he will pass along. The power and energy you take with you into a presentation is lost; that is why it is particularly important to have strong support material.

Find out how many people are on the committee, prepare a folder for each member with all of the written information you wish him to have; then let samples, pictures, charts, and graphs do your talking.

An old axiom in sales is "Plan your work—and work your plan." As tired as that expression is, it still makes a world of sense. The salespeople who fail to plan and prepare for every call are doomed to mediocrity. The lack of preparation, the failure to plan, becomes crystal clear to the prospect. He is offended: an unprepared, unplanned presentation shows a lack of respect for him and his time. Time is something the salesperson cannot waste. Every salesperson should jealously guard his time and the time of his prospect.

Would you believe that some salespeople plan their day and week, think about every account they will see and how they will sell them, set goals, and then completely abandon their plans when they get before the buyer? They plan their work—but they do not work their plan. There is no value in this. If your plan is properly researched, you can have confidence it will work. Stick to the plan.

Chapter 15

The Cold Call

The very expression cold call seems intimidating, impersonal, and unfriendly. Making calls on strangers may seem scary. You don't know what to expect, you don't know who to talk to, and you may go through a bit of a hassle until you find the decision maker. But remember, when you make cold calls, you can exercise the entire sales procedure, from the warm-up to the close. This is a wonderful way to keep sharp, to stay on your toes, and to sharpen your skills.

Some salespeople hate making cold calls because they think it is demeaning. "I feel more like a street peddler or a beggar than I do a salesman," my star rookie once told me. "I talked with the buyer at one account, and he denied he was the buyer. I knew he was, but what could I say? It was just so humiliating." I could relate to that; some people are so insecure they will avoid meeting salespeople and hope to avoid having to make decisions.

"Larry," I told him, "the secret to making cold calls is attitude. You must be quietly aggressive. You must bring a thick skin and a sense of humor with you, and you have to accept the fact that some people will abuse their positions of authority and treat all visitors in a rude, unbusinesslike way. Your established accounts behave in the same way sometimes—isn't that true? Some are friendly and honest, while others are gruff, rude, and dishonest." Larry agreed that that was indeed true.

I have devised a list of attitude adjustments that every salesperson about to make cold calls should take to heart. Review these and perhaps other ideas will come to you as you do so.

1. Believe the call you make will result in your making a business friend. Say that to yourself before you make every cold call.

2. Say, "I am enthusiastic about my company and its products (or service). Everyone needs my product and will want to know all I can tell them about it."

3. Say, "I'm going to see humor in a silly buyer's attitude or behavior. If he tries to hide from me, I will find him—and have fun doing it."

4. Say, "I will not take no for an answer without an explanation from the buyer. I will dig deep for information that can be used to show why he needs my products."

5. Say, "I will not be overly sensitive. If the buyer cannot see me, there is probably a good reason. I will then arrange an appointment and gather as much information as I can to help me when I honor that appointment."

If you know what you are going to do and what you hope to achieve with every call, your success ratio will be greatly improved. Attitude and enthusiasm will carry the day, and remember, without a transfusion of new prospects, your business will dry up. You need to make cold calls; it is important to your growth and it can be fun.

A good day of cold calling must start with preparation.

1. Determine what area you intend to cover and draw up a temporary itinerary. Knowing where the accounts are will eliminate frustration, make your day go by faster, and allow you to cover more ground.

2. Examine the list of potential prospects and eliminate those you are sure cannot become accounts: poor credit risks; accounts that are too small and cannot buy your minimum order; those too big for you to serve; any captive account (subsidiary companies who are supplied by parent companies); and all accounts outside your assigned area.

3. Develop an introduction for yourself. Instead of "Mr. Prospect, my name is Harry Greenberg, and I represent Big Trends Company . . ." have something that will grab the interest of the prospect immediately, such as "Mr. Prospect, I have a product that can save your company thousands of dollars in maintenance costs every year. It's proven, guaranteed, and underpriced.

Can I take a few minutes of your time to explain how it works?"

RESISTANCE

Sometimes you have to climb over receptionists, secretaries, assistants, or others to get to the buyer. This can shorten your temper and end up making you say or do something that will preclude you from ever getting business from the account. Face these people with honesty.

You don't know who the buyer is, so treat everyone you talk to as you would the buyer. Honesty is the best policy. Never try to disguise your mission. Respond to "Can I help you?" honestly and in depth. "My name is Harry Greenberg. I represent Big Trends Company, and I'd like a few minutes of the buyer's time. Could you tell me his name and how I can reach him?" Sometimes this is followed by a "What does this regard" question. Tell her. "My company has a product that can reduce maintenance costs by thousands of dollars each year, and I'd like to discuss it with the buyer." You might be surprised to know that these defenders really want to help! "Oh, you're in the wrong building; Mr. Smits buys all maintenance supplies and systems. He's in building 10-A, just across the quadrangle."

Use common sense in making cold calls. Most businessmen are busy in the mornings until about 10 o'clock and in the late afternoon, after 3. Housewives, who can make appointments for their husbands, are busy fixing breakfast and getting the kids off to school until about 9:30. They are usually free to talk to you until about 2, when the youngsters are out of school. Construction accounts like early morning appointments, while professional people (doctors, dentists, lawyers, and accountants), usually post office hours, and you can call on them within those limits. Good timing can, of course, be an important factor in making your cold calling day a success or failure.

Being open, friendly, and honest is the only way to overcome resistance, but some salespeople make a mistake by investing too much importance in the secretary, receptionist, or assistant. They're not the buyers, and you will do well not to forget that. Enlist their help, let them know what you want to accomplish, but never take a no from them as a final answer. "I don't think we'd be interested," the secretary says in a dismissing way. "When a buyer understands our program, he becomes very interested. Would you please see if he is available?" is your answer.

First-time interviews are sometimes granted out of courtesy. The buyer is busy with telephone calls, answering correspondence, or some other time-intensive duty. He invites you in just to be a nice guy and to get rid of you on good terms. He shakes hands, motions to a chair, and then continues reading a report.

Remember that you are at a disadvantage to begin with: this is a cold call. You are a stranger, he has never heard of you or your product, and you need his total attention if your visit is to be fruitful. Don't say a word until he puts the report aside and pays attention. He might say, "Go on, I'm listening," but don't do it. Instead, either offer to come back at a time when he can give you the necessary attention, or tell him, "Mr. Prospect, I can see you are busy, as I am, but this opportunity deserves your full attention. Please continue reading your report, and then we'll visit." What does this do? It assigns value to your visit, it gives you a measure of control, and it establishes dignity.

While talking to one of my salespeople about cold-calling techniques, he said that when the buyer continues to do something other than give him his total attention, he simply lowers his voice. "They usually put aside whatever they are doing, and pay attention." It may have worked for him, but I don't recommend it. In an earlier chapter, I told the story of a salesman who inadvertently dropped his voice during an interview. It was an annoying habit and it ruined his sales. Lowering one's voice is a ploy that works in group meetings but not in one-on-one interviews. If you drop your voice during a meeting that wasn't scheduled and in which the prospect may not recognize the importance of, you can be sure he will simply tune out.

TURNING GRIPES INTO GRINS

Cold calling is only one way to find new business. Another way is networking. We've all heard of the old-boy network. But the network I'm talking about is the existing list of happy customers you already have. Company A does business with Company B. Company A is your customer, but you can't get started with Company B. Talk to your happy customer. Ask him to arrange an interview with B. Ask him to pick up the telephone and call B while you're still in his office. That is strong medicine and overcomes many obstacles.

Some fraternal organizations, professional societies, and social clubs can be good sources for business. The trick here is not to be too aggressive. Nothing turns a prospect off faster than believing his friendship is being solicited for ulterior motives. A friend of mine recently offered to arrange a golf game with the CEO of a major chain operation. This organization is one of the largest in the west, and the CEO turned out to be a warm and friendly fellow with a great sense of humor and a wicked slice. We hit it off very well until I started talking about how my products would benefit his stores. "Bill," he said in a friendly but unmistakable way, "I never get in the way of my buyers. I'm sure you can understand why." That was it! He had said it all. Later, after the game and enjoying a drink in the clubhouse, he took me aside and promised to make sure I could present my program in the best way possible.

This executive felt he had been cornered. I really believed we could be a value to his stores, but I had rushed the entire process. If I had simply enjoyed the day, and allowed things to take their natural course, this gentleman would have asked me what I did for a living, and how he could help me. I didn't and he didn't.

Credit and service problems can be a rich source of leads and increased business. I always like to receive a notice that this account or that was delinquent by thirty days or more. I figure they were either having a problem with our company or the merchandise I sold them. Why else would an otherwise creditworthy company suddenly refuse to pay? Sure enough, nine times out of ten, they had a bone stuck in their throats—overshipped, undershipped, mis-billed, damaged goods, something that made them say, "I'll show them, I just won't pay." When you solve problems like these, the buyer naturally feels obligated. Sometimes they also feel a bit contrite for having made a mountain out of a molehill. What better time to ask for more business or an introduction to another account?

Service problems, like credit problems, present opportunities to turn gripes into grins. Never avoid problems with your product. If it doesn't work—get it fixed, quickly and completely. Even if you authorize a return of merchandise, which may cost you a temporary loss of commissions, you have solved a problem and assured your customer you are interested in his welfare. That is a deposit of goodwill that cannot be gained in any other way.

When calling on accounts for the first time, you will frequently hear powerful and pointed objections to your product. One buyer told a salesperson of mine, "Your products are interesting and of excellent quality, but they are just too expensive. My customers won't pay that much for vitamins. I've been in this business for years, and I know my customers."

The salesman answered, "Mr. Buyer, when people come into your store, they don't come here for vitamins, they come in because they want to feel better. They come here to solve problems they are having with their health. If you sell them formulas that are only marginally effective, or not effective at all, they won't come back. But if they get results, they become your best advertising, they rave about your store, they introduce others to the vitamins that have worked so well for them—and you have a customer for life. People will pay for what works, make no mistake. If they feel better and have more energy, they will pay any reasonable price—and our products work." The answer was given with so much honesty and sincerity that the buyer had no choice but to accept it without argument. When someone tells you your product is priced too high, think of this response and see if you can adapt it.

"No one knows your product. It isn't advertised," a buyer said on another occasion.

"I admit it," the salesperson answered. "And that is why we are able to offer our product for less. We don't have the high cost of advertising and slick packaging. I'm sure there are many customers who will seek out the highly advertised product you mention, but I'm equally sure there are a great number who want a product of high quality that will fit into their budget. Are you willing to surrender that segment of the market?" It was a clever answer and one that didn't allow a no response. Remember, all products have their reason to exist—high quality, price, endurance/strength, fad, style, effectiveness—you must discover which reason best fits your product; therein lie the answers to buyers' objections.

Many times a new buyer will resist changing to a new supplier because it is too much trouble or it is a risk. "I don't know your stuff, but I know XYZ's;been with them for years, and they are reliable. I just don't see the advantage in switching; there isn't that much to gain," the industrial buyer says. But what was he really saying? The salesperson felt the buyer was only asking for affirmation. The salesman was prepared. He withdrew a stack of letters of recommendation from prominent customers, people who used and highly recommended the product. "These are letters from people who know my product and are happy with it. We didn't pay for them to write the letters. They wanted to share what they had learned with others." Cleverly, he added "Advertising is paid for; anyone can buy advertising."

"I like your stuff, but XYZ gives me a bigger margin of profit," the buyer said. "Are you more interested in margin or money?" the salesperson replied. "Here, let me show you the difference," and taking a pencil and paper, he showed how one might make a bigger margin of profit, but fewer profit dollars. It was an eyeopener to the buyer, who resisted the logic he saw. But eventually, he came around.

Remember the answers given here, adapt them to your own situation, think of others, and be prepared to answer the most frequent objections. As I've said, there are reasons for every product on the marketplace. When they outlive their value and utility, they are discarded. But as long as a category is being used, every product in the category has a place and can be sold. Know your product and your market, and the answers will come to you.

Chapter 16

Selling Sense

Buyers become jaded after a time; for this reason, merchandise managers switch them from category to category. Still, they get tired of hearing more or less the same speech from salesperson after salesperson. We've mentioned the need for grabbing the buyer's attention in the first few minutes; having a lead-in that will arrest his attention and make him want to know more. Most sales managers will stress the importance of telling the buyer the benefits his company will derive from buying this product or that, but even that becomes hackneyed after a while. The buyer develops an I've-heard-this-before attitude, and the salesperson never really gets to the meat of his presentation.

Salespeople go to great lengths to devise openings that will get the buyer to pay attention to them and the easiest method is to appeal to their senses. "Mr. Buyer, I'm going to *show* you an interesting product that is new to the market, but first I want you to *feel* the difference between these two fabrics" is the kind of opening that immediately gets the buyer involved in your presentation. He will touch the product—which some contend transfers ownership—and will want to know more. Even if he gives a negative reply, "I don't feel any difference" a dialogue is started. "You don't feel the difference? Most people do immediately, but let me *show* you why this is different from any fabric you have in your store." Now you take the fabric, and draw his visual sense towards the sample. "Can you *see* the difference in texture and can you *see* the close weave?" He will closely examine the fabric, perhaps attempting to find a way to discredit your sample. Don't be afraid of that, he is just fishing, trying to determine if his objections have merit. He wants to be convinced. If you are prepared, if you can answer his objections, you'll make the sale.

Bringing the senses into the presentation is possible in almost any situation. "You can barely *hear* the engine, isn't that true?" "*Smell* the rich chocolate baked into these cookies; doesn't that remind you of your grandmother's kitchen?" Similar questions and suggestions will motivate your buyer's interest and get him involved.

Naturally, when a buyer is considering two or more products, he will make various tests. He might ask people in his office for their opinions or ask his spouse or children what they think, so it only makes good sense to get a dramatic demonstration that might be entertaining as well as informative. For instance, a friend of mine, selling an orange-flavored drink, was having a tough time getting it into grocery stores and chains. His product was tasty, rich in vitamins and minerals, and looked just like fresh-squeezed orange juice. But the competition was a huge, nationally known and advertised product. My friend's promotional budget was limited and he was stuck on dead center, until one evening he saw an ad on TV about the aroma of coffee. In the ad, a college kid was returning home early one morning for Christmas vacation. Greeted by his baby brother, the two tiptoed into the kitchen and brewed coffee. The aroma of fresh-brewed coffee awakened the parents, and a warm family scene was enacted.

"Why couldn't my orange-flavored breakfast drink do the same sort of thing?" Naturally, the smell of orange-flavored drinks will not fill the air as will coffee, but a blindfold test would work. He brought in his product and three competitor's products along with paper cups and a blindfold. "My product looks and tastes like freshly squeezed oranges, and even more impressive—it *smells* like it, too." Pouring out the competitor's products and a cup of his drink, he asked the buyer to put on a blindfold. He would let him judge which drink *smelled* like fresh oranges.

The buyer thought it was a little silly—but fun, too, so he went along. Needless to say, he picked my friend's product—as did several other people in the office. Now I don't know how many people buy an orange drink because it *smells* like fresh oranges, but the buyer did. Senses make sense.

Illustrating and demonstrating what your product will do can be very powerful and can bring a message home in a strong yet lighthearted way. Several years ago a colleague of mine was introducing a weight-loss formula. This is an extremely crowded, competitive field, filled with large companies who spend millions of dollars on advertising. My friend couldn't compete with these giants, and didn't want to; instead he would settle for a small slice of a huge pie. If he could show that his diet product worked, he could sell on that basis and on its lower price.

My friend had a weight problem. Standing only 5'7" tall, he weighed almost 225 pounds! Those are dangerous dimensions, and an absolute killer to someone trying to sell diet products, so my friend decided to take his own product and lose some weight. The next time I saw him, I barely recognized him! He was 165 pounds and looked great—except for one thing. His clothes hung on him like a tarpaulin; he looked ridiculous. He could turn his head without his shirt moving at all since his neck was fifteen inches and the shirt was seventeen. His trousers were so baggy he reminded me of a circus clown. "Bobby, you look great, but . . ." I never got to finish my sentence.

"I know. I feel like a nitwit, but I have a call to make on chain headquarters today. The buyer hasn't seen me since last summer when I first tried to sell him my formula, and he turned me down flat. This is my way of showing him that it works," he said. I pointed out that wearing a smart-looking suit might illustrate the point just as well, but he insisted this was more dramatic, and that buyers are always so impressed they call others in to show him off. "I haven't missed a sale since I started using this prop," he said. And he was right.

This example is not extreme. We all know that television advertising sells products; what is that, if it isn't demonstrating and illustrating? A leading diaper manufacturer illustrates how his product absorbs moisture, a shaving cream maker demonstrates how his product prevents razor burn, and so on. Whatever your product or service, it will probably lend itself to demonstration using the five senses. Think how you might enjoy the sense in verbalizing or actually demonstrating your merchandise.

Packaging also has a powerful influence on the consumer's buying habits. Some years ago a popular syrup was sold in containers that looked like tiny backwoods cabins. This product is now sold in bottles like other syrups, but the backwoods cabin container did its job and established this syrup as one of the nation's leading sellers. Vitamin makers have discovered that selling one-a-day vitamin packs in cans leads the consumer to believe the cans contain powders, since so many powders come in cans. They have also learned that for some reason consumers shy away from buying any vitamin formula packaged in a box! As a salesperson, you may not have the power to change packaging, but it is your responsibility to feed that information to the home office along with your recommendations.

CROSS-SELLING

Many times an opportunity to increase sales is right under our noses but we are too busy to recognize it. Cross-selling refers to tying together two or more products and selling them in tandem. In the food business, for instance, Chinese food is sometimes packaged so that fried noodles are shrink-wrapped to a can of chop suey. The two are used together, so why not sell them together? Well, I could give at least a half dozen reasons why that doesn't make good marketing sense, but from another standpoint there is some value in this idea. Not so long ago a prominent manufacturer of photo lenses and electronic flashes took the Chinese food idea and packaged its new telephoto lens with an adapter. Together, the adapter and lens doubled the focal length of the lens. It was a remarkably clever idea and sold well.

Products do not have to be physically tied to each other to be sold together. Eggs are often displayed near bacon, ham, and other breakfast meats. Shirts are displayed near neckties, socks near the shoe department, and golf balls close to golf clubs. In short, the merchandiser utilizes the impulse factor the shopper is likely to have. His primary purchase may be skis, but a parka might be tacked onto the sale if it is displayed nearby. How can you use cross-selling to increase your sales and broaden your product base?

Think of the benefits your product delivers to the consumer and consider other products in your line that might naturally follow. The buyer, always alert for new merchandising ideas, will be interested in hearing your ideas. He may trim it and shape it to fit his particular need, and he might make suggestions that add immeasurably to the success of your idea.

Don't be afraid to be bold in marketing your product. Many buyers will lack the vision and imagination necessary to see the possibilities, but when you meet the promoter, the type that makes things happen, your search will be well worthwhile.

ROUTINE = BORING

The thing I like most about selling is the constantly changing challenges before you. New buyers with different ideas and different approaches are always coming on the scene. New companies are forcing their way into the market, and new products are always being presented. Yesterday's leaders can be today's also-rans. It's tough to be bored in sales, and yet I have salespeople ask me, "I can't get excited about my job; how do you manage to stay motivated?"

Having kids in college helps, but money isn't the only motivator. Napoleon said, "Men will die for a piece of ribbon." Actually they don't die for the ribbon, but for the accolades of their comrades. All sales people are motivated by accolades. The money is important, of course, but being the best and judged as such by one's peers is true motivation.

But how can this information help you with your self-motivation. In this way: Before every call, say to yourself

1. I am totally prepared to make this call. I know everything about my product (or service). I know who I am selling against and have matched my strengths against theirs. I have considered all possible objections I might hear and have solid arguments that will convince the buyer that mine is the right product for him.
2. I have a prepared presentation that *creates* and *identifies* need, and I can show how my product will fill that need.
3. I have all back-up materials to support my presentation, including samples, point-of-sale materials, and consumer literature.
4. No buyer can withstand my power presentation. *I am the best there is.*
5. The buyer will recognize the value of my product and will be happy to see me.

Do some or perhaps all of these points seem a bit silly? Well, none of them are. I *know* they work.

Motivational experts advise people to tape to the mirror in the bathroom similar boosters. They want you to see in writing the goals you set for yourself every morning—a reminder of what you should focus on. It is so easy to become unfocused, so easy to forget what you are trying to achieve.

All I ask is that you try this small motivational-focusing method for just thirty days—thirty working days. Carefully read the list before every call and think about the meaning of each point. At the end of thirty days, your improvement will be so marked, that you will continue without my urging. My hope is you will pass the idea along to someone else who needs a little motivational help.

There is a certain monotony and routine in every job, even a territory sales job. Recently one of my salespeople pointed out, "You're always pushing us to stay to our itinerary, but that's boring and routine. I don't want to be a route salesperson, I want to spread my wings!" The guy's a poet and he has a point. Calling on the same accounts on a regular basis is rather mundane, but only to the degree that you allow it to be so.

If you approach every call as being a unique and separate entity, you will discover that they are just that. They may buy the same products but they serve different kinds of consumers, their goals are different, and the plan for reaching those goals are very different. If you learn who your customers are (and by that I mean what they are trying to achieve), you can devise programs that will assist them in reaching their goals—you will truly serve their needs.

Devising these promotional schemes is, at least for me, the most enjoyable part of my job. Selling should be fun. If you don't enjoy what you're doing, analyze and discover why. If you like selling, but you're not happy with what you're selling, change jobs. I'd rather be unemployed than working at some task that bored me to death. Think of it this way: Suppose you knew you only had forty hours to live. What would you do with those forty hours? Most people would go to church, visit relatives, spend as much time as they could with family and friends, and prepare for the end. I can't think of anyone who would honestly say they would go to work. No one knows how much longer he has, so every hour should be as pleasurable as possible. Obviously that doesn't mean that every day is New Year's Eve, but it should be interesting, fun, challenging, and exciting. You are the architect of your future. Build a good one.

Chapter 17

Overview: The Customer Is Always . . . the Customer

I always get a little nauseated when I hear someone say, "The customer is always right." I know what they are really saying: the power is always with the customer. That's true enough. As for them being always right, well, the fact is they are frequently wrong. However, right or wrong, the wise salesperson will never try to prove a customer or protentional customer either. If you prove the buyer wrong, the chances of making the sale are diminished. If you prove him right, you lose the sale, so either way you lose. But selling isn't a test of wits or a contest to determine who is the smarter; rather, selling is the art of persuasion. Remember that. Being right is the aim of the sales introvert; getting the sale is the aim of the salesperson. I have stressed throughout this book the importance of knowing what you want to accomplish. If your goals are clearly defined and your focus is turned toward reaching those goals, winning a point or an argument will be unimportant.

In this final chapter, we will review some of the most important points from previous chapters. You may wish to use this part of the book as a quick refresher course when the need arises.

❖ ❖ ❖

Dealing with people can be very difficult. You never know what is going on in their lives: illness, financial loss, marriage problems, insecurity in their jobs, all sorts of things—any or all of which can and do affect the way they treat you and others. When you are trying to sell something, you are trying to make someone decide in your favor.

Look at it this way: The buyer is sitting in his office, enjoying his morning coffee, and trying to decide where he will have lunch. Things are tranquil and quiet—just the way he likes them—when you show up. This means a complete change of his routine. He has things pretty well the way he wants them, business is good, everything is smooth, and now he must make a decision! If he decides yes, it will mean a mountain of paperwork, justification to his boss, all sorts of adjustments. If the answer is no, the salesperson will want an explanation. It may be a long day. No wonder buyers are sometimes hostile. So: how do you change that attitude?

First of all, remember the mechanical rules of selling:

◆ *The warm-up.* Break the ice; let him know you are a person.
◆ *The qualification.* Make sure he is the right person you should be talking to.
◆ *The presentation.* Make sure you *never* sell a product. Sell an idea, sell a concept, and always, always, create a need for your product or service.
◆ *The close.* Remember the close doesn't necessarily happen at the end. Close early and often.
◆ *The after-close.* Not always used, but a vital part of the sale in some circumstances. Remember, an after-close can be a letter or a simple note.

Remember, too, that emotion drives all sales. A buyer is interested in the logical, factual features of a product, but emotion will make him buy. Touch the emotion and you power the sale. Every product has an emotional appeal; find it and you find the secret of closing.

Make your presentation exciting, filled with words that motivate and inspire. Memorize the twelve power words, and use them in your presentation and especially in your close. Be prepared for whatever objections your prospect may throw at you. On your own, play the devil's advocate to your own product. This is one of the best ways to discover what objections you will face. Use props, support materials, and samples. Use gestures, voice inflections, and endorsements. Be so well informed about your products and your competitor's products that buyers will want to hear more, will ask questions, and will sell themselves.

Learn to listen. Listening is the most powerful tool a salesperson has. Listening will tell you what the buyer wants, what features are most important to him, and *how* you can sell him. If you learn when to shut up, the buyer will often sell himself.

Develop a dialogue with the buyer. Make him a part of your presentation. Remember, when they talk, they don't walk. The simplest way to start a dialogue is to ask questions—questions that require opinions, an exchange of ideas, even a vehement denial. Ask questions throughout your presentation. Ask questions and harvest affirmations as you funnel your presentation toward a close. The more yeses you harvest, the easier and the bigger the sale. When you run into a bump in the road, an objection when you ask for affirmation, welcome it. It gives you a chance to strengthen your cause, to develop your presentation, to use the props, samples, and other support materials. "No" often means he is listening and interested! When a buyer fights against your strongest selling points, he is often saying, "I'm interested or I wouldn't bother to argue. I want to believe you. Convince me." Questions will make the hidden reasons surface.

Don't be afraid to close. Closing is the essence of selling. You *want* a decision. You have worked to get one. If the answer is yes, the battle is over—in most cases. Remember, only a tiny part of your work week is spent with a decision make but it is the most important part of your work week. All of your planning and preparation is aimed at putting you in position to get an answer. If the answer is no, the battle has just begun. Don't accept rejection until you know why. You are entitled to know why you have been refused. The buyer's answer may not be—and in most cases is not—final. Circle back to the beginning if possible. Ask questions and more questions. This is where the fun begins; this is where your skills are honed. When you turn a no into a yes, you will feel wonderful.

The successful territory salesperson will create and maintain careful records. Records are not a burden; being without records is. As I mentioned, an itinerary will increase sales as much as 35 percent. Update your itinerary as needed, but never discard it. Knowing where you should be every day gives you direction and purpose. Keep a record of every account, even if you don't do business with them. An account record is a picture of the account when you are away; don't trust your memory. Know what you promised and what was promised you; know what you sold on your last visit and set goals for your next.

Never avoid problems with your product or service. When products back up in a store, *bring it to the attention of the buyer and demand to know why it isn't selling!* Ignoring the problem will only make the problem bigger and probably unsolvable. Resell the product, remind the buyer why he bought it, why it has merit, and show him how to sell it successfully in his store.

Be innovative. Learn to develop programs and promotions that add zest to the retailer's business and add dollars to his bottom line. Don't forget, selling in a product is often only half the job. The other half is seeing that it sells out. Your obligation to the buyer doesn't end until he has enjoyed a profit from the goods you sold him. Help him to sell.

Make sure you teach and train the retail salespeople just as you do the buyer. The retail salesperson can be a strong ally or a powerful enemy. Treat everyone with respect and be interested in what they do. Today's clerk may be tomorrow's buyer.

Don't get so wrapped up in your own endeavors that you forget that buyers have a difficult, demanding, and stress-filled job. Respect their time, make your visit worth his while, and be prepared. At the same time, remember that you are doing an important job, providing a vital service, and without you business could not exist. You deserve respect. You are not a beggar or a peddler; you are a salesperson—one of the oldest professions in the world and the highest paid profession in America. Keep an air of dignity about you without being stiff or unnecessarily formal.

Remember you learn from every sales contact you make. Take the time to examine every sales call and ask yourself just that—what did I learn? Make notes of what you have learned and how you can improve.

Make the buyer your business friend, but resist becoming a personal friend. It is much easier to say no to a friend than it is to a stranger. The salesperson will become frustrated and will begin depending on friendship instead of his selling skills, and that is a formula for disaster. Becoming too close will cause compromises on your part and on the part of the buyer; it will be a strain on your relationship and can have damaging results. Familiarity often breeds contempt, and the formality of the office or store is a useful and valuable barrier that should not be struck down.

Entertaining is sometimes a necessary part of sales, and it is best done at group functions. Gift giving should be limited to small, business-oriented items that remind the buyer of you and your company. Gifts should not exceed fifty dollars.

Remember, an introvert is someone who wants to be right. An extrovert wants to be liked. Most of us have a little of each characteristic in us, but all will have a tendency to learn toward being an introvert or extrovert. If you can identify your buyer as being one or the other, your sales presentation, directed towards his tendency, will be successful most of the time.

A salesperson doesn't fit any specific mold. Like buyers, they come in all shapes and sizes, all genders and colors. Some are introverts and others are extroverts. You can develop a sales personality, but you have to realize not everyone is meant to be in sales. If you don't enjoy selling, it can be a crushing, burdensome job. Be wise enough to recognize where your talents lie, and know what you like doing. If sales isn't for you, do something else; contentment and other rewards will follow.

Don't fear making new contacts, searching out new prospects, or making cold calls. If you prepare carefully and carry the proper attitude, you'll find cold calling can be an interesting, even enjoyable experience. Be honest, open, and frank with people who place themselves between you and the decision maker. Enlist them in your cause. Trying to deceive them can only cause ill feeling and hostility. Join social clubs, fraternal organizations, and professional groups for the pleasure and sense of community you can gain—never for the business you may generate.

It may seem like an overwhelming list of things a salesperson must know and do, and I agree it is formidable. However, experience is the best of all teachers. Following the rules set forth in this book will help you along your way. If you master what I have tried to teach you, you will know how to sell the tough buyer. A salesperson has many things to do, many things to learn, many skills to master—but the most important quality he must have is honesty. Good luck.